# DECOR

## DECORATING THE NEW AUSTRALIAN WAY

AUSTRALIAN

# HOUSE
## &GARDEN

# DECOR
## DECORATING THE NEW AUSTRALIAN WAY

ACPbooks

# CREATING A HOME

Decorating unleashes your creativity and the whole wonderful process can be great fun. It's not just about keeping up with fashion and its many and varied cycles; it's about making a home where both you and your family will always feel comfortable and happy.    In decorating, a touch of bravado can reap huge rewards – yes, rules are sometimes meant to be broken, or at the very least bent a little. Experimenting will give you a home that proclaims 'this is me and this is mine!'.    DECOR shows you where to begin to create your nest. This latest book from *Australian House & Garden* magazine takes you on a journey of discovery through the best choices for walls, floors, furniture and more, drawing them into rooms made for modern living.    Mix and match what suits you best. A home isn't about showroom perfection – it's about creating a place for love and laughter.

# BEGINNINGS 8

Walls, floors and windows form the structural base of any decorating scheme. Staircases and fireplaces are the other built-in elements that will influence your decor.

# NECESSITIES 52

Storage, lighting and having your place wired for new technology aren't afterthoughts. Decide on what you need and build it in as soon as you can for a smooth-running home.

# DECORATION 80

What you embellish your home's structural base with gives your nest heart and soul. It's the little things as well as the big-ticket items that add punch and personality.

# CONTENTS

## COMFORT 108

Comfort should be at the core of your sanctuary. Make it as inviting as possible with sofas to dive into, places to chat and an easygoing style. The more you relax, the more you enjoy.

## LIVING 138

How you live should be reflected in your everyday rooms. Tailor your home to suit a 21st-century lifestyle. Meld indoors with out and decorate to catch the breeze.

In the huge entertaining area of a contemporary waterside mansion, innovative design brings together some unusual touches. Japanese 'shoji-inspired' columns, kwila timber cabinetry and vibrant fabrics put a surprise element in every corner.

Decorating is a journey of discovery and fulfilment. But before you begin, and certainly before you buy anything, take a good hard look at the basic elements of a room. The space itself should always be assessed in the most critical way. This means looking beyond the existing furnishings to the primary structure of walls, floors, windows and doors, and dominant architectural features like a staircase or fireplace. Only by being fully informed will you be confident about making the right decisions… and the best choices. And this is just the beginning.

# STYLING THE WALLS

YOU CAN EITHER DRAW ATTENTION TO YOUR WALLS OR SIMPLY USE THEM AS
A BACKDROP TO YOUR OTHER FURNISHINGS, BUT HOW YOU CHOOSE TO COLOUR
THEM IN – BE IT WITH PAINT, PATTERN OR TEXTURED MATERIALS – DETERMINES
HOW DECORATIVE THE ROOM WILL BE. EXPLORE THE OPTIONS.

### 1. PLAY UP AN ALCOVE

An alcove or recessed wall
becomes the focus of a room
when it's treated in a special
way. You can display artworks
or collectables by staging them
against a dominant colour. Paint
the recess in a warm or dark
colour and it will recede even
further, giving added depth to
the room. In this formal dining
area, the recess is painted in
a dense red and the buffet fits
neatly into the space.

Walls dominate the look of a room for
one simple reason – they are the largest
surface in that area. You can't escape their
impact; they enclose a room or break up
the space in an open-plan layout.

But think beyond the walls being
a boundary, and you will discover some
exciting decorating possibilities. Walls
can provide the visual link between one
room and the next, or be the background
to a focal point within a room.

Home decorators are spoiled for choice
when it comes to materials and finishes
for walls – from paint, paper and fabric
to tile, wood panelling, mirror and glass.
However it's a wall's colour that most
immediately gives a room its look.

The rules are pretty straightforward: if
you want the walls to dissolve into the
background, then you should gravitate
towards neutrals and solid colours and
avoid textured finishes. But for greater
impact, use patterns and stronger colours
to give more clout to the walls.

If you haven't thought about what will
go against the walls then you're heading
into trouble, because any paintings or
imposing pieces of furniture will need to
complement your wall colours. But if
what is going on or against the walls is
not an issue, then how you decorate
them comes back to personal preference.

## CHOOSING COLOURS

Colour is decorating's most powerful tool.
With a sweep of the paintbrush, colour
can transform a melange of architectural

## 2. UNITING WITH COLOUR

Industrial and commercial conversions respond like magic to large splashes of brilliant colour. It's often used as a device to unify irregularly shaped walls and odd floor levels and window heights. Colour and texture go hand in hand in this home, which began life as a corner pub and milk bar. The designer wanted to add warmth and has used a fiery combo of yellow and red applied with a circular brush technique to create a textured finish.

and furnishing styles into a cohesive whole. But it's all too easy to get carried away with a 'decorating dream' that turns out to be hard to live with on a day-to-day basis. (Particularly seductive is the slick chic of a very pale scheme, frequently associated with the minimalist look. Although attractive, such a scheme can be maintained only by those with an orderly and fastidious nature.)

Stick with a colour palette you truly love, not what's trendy. Think in terms of colour groups such as earthy, marine or monochromatic. And remember that often the particular shade you choose is more crucial than the basic colour. In the end, the only legitimate basis for choosing colours is that you feel happy with them.

## USING COLOUR IN THE HOME

One way of viewing colour is to identify the warm and cool colours. Warm colours advance (think of red, yellow and orange and those containing more red than blue),

as do dark colours; cool colours recede (blue and green and those with more blue than red). Pale colours also recede.

Knowing this you can create colour schemes that address specific problems. For example, you can use colour to alter the proportions of a room (such as visually lowering or raising a ceiling), to disguise awkwardly-shaped rooms, to create an illusion of space or to give a room an intimate, cosy ambience.

Colour won't work without light, and the amount and sort of light that a room receives can either bring a colour to life or flatten it dead. You'll find that the cold light from the south is better suited to warm colours. Brilliant light from the east and north can be tempered with cooler colours.

The surrounding environment also has an effect. Light in built-up areas is more diffused than that found in open country. Buildings that are very close can also reflect unwanted colour into a room.

### 1. ATTENTION GETTERS

A wall's defining moment is when it serves to draw attention to what it is enclosing. This beach-house bathroom can be wholly concealed by a steel roller shutter, partly hidden by a coloured canvas blind, or be totally opened up to the courtyard. The curved wall enables the toilet to be located outside the wet area.

### 2. USE GLASS FOR GLOSS

Glass has always been valued for its translucency, and in contemporary design you will see glass floors, glass basins and now walls panelled in glass. The effect is cutting edge. Glass can be painted any colour and when fixed to the wall gives it a fabulous glossy appearance. In this kitchen, the glass on the wall has been colour-coded to the resin benchtop and funky dining chairs.

## 3. CREATING A FEATURE

Often in decorating you have to turn a negative into a positive. When the owners of this home renovated, they were stuck with a pillar which dominated their living room; they could neither move nor hide it. So they opted to make it a highlight by turning it into a display and storage unit. Painted white to give it emphasis against a deep blue feature wall, it works superbly.

1  2

3

Think about climate, too – the bright colours that are so at ease in the tropics will appear garish in the softer, more angled light of southern climes.

Artificial light also has a tricky effect on colour, making certain shades appear dirty or dull. Paint a sample board to see how a colour actually looks in a room before committing it to the walls.

## EMOTIONS AND COLOUR

Certain colours uplift and excite, while others calm and pacify. And as colour affects your mood, it makes sense to consider colour psychology when you're putting together a scheme. In places of great activity, like the kitchen, you would use a warm colour because it relates to the high energy levels. But in a place where you want to relax, select a cool colour like blue or green (avoid the red-based blues).

4

### 1. DEFINE YOUR ZONES

Floor plans today are certainly more open, but there is still a need to define different zones. Blade walls break an open-plan space but avoid giving it a confined feeling. Here, a dividing 'wall' delineates the kitchen. Finished in black mosaic tiles, it adds texture to the room. A bold red feature wall, punctuated with backlit voids, signals the dining station.

### 2. MAKE AN ENTRANCE

In many apartments, the entry opens directly into the living room, but to give an entrance privacy by closing it in with a solid wall would compromise light and space. The owner of this high-rise apartment came up with the solution of screening the area with a combination of opaque and clear glass panels; the clear 'window' treats guests to the impressive view right from the front door.

### 3. USING MIRRORS

An expanse of mirror multiplies the effect of natural light and is an inconspicuous but very practical decorating tool. In this renovated apartment, the designer has made living 'pictures' of two full-size mirrors by framing them with aluminium trim and mounting them separately out from the wall.

### 4. SLICE UP A VIEW

You can add intrigue to a room by breaking into the walls to create see-through vignettes or vistas – but leave load-bearing walls alone. A series of niches in this aubergine-painted wall gives a staggered view across the hall to the kitchen and informal living room.

### STARTING TO COMBINE COLOURS

This is the fun bit. An easy way to start is to limit yourself to three colours. But using these properly means thinking about the proportions in which they are to be featured. If you're scared stiff about putting a strong colour on the walls, go for neutral walls with a bolder colour as a highlight on the woodwork or on a feature wall. You can also try a scheme with different tones and shades of the one hue for a harmonious effect.

### USING PATTERN AND TEXTURE

Pattern, like colour, can create anxiety in those who aren't used to playing the mix-and-match game. This is particularly the case when it comes to mixing fabric patterns. But if you want to add depth and visual richness to a decorating scheme, nothing can compete with pattern on a large scale. Whether it's a feature column surfaced in tile, or a feature wall papered in a delicate pearl foil paper, pattern is what makes colour come alive.

Examine most decorating styles and you'll discover that pattern and texture are integral to the look. Moroccan style, for example, has a brilliant palette, but it's the intricate mosaic tile patterns which focus attention on the colour.

Today, you can cover a wall in virtually anything. Glass panels, exotic timber veneers, bamboo sheeting, tile, metal mesh and metal coatings create their own patterns (and texture) when they are combined. By being adventurous and confident with pattern and texture, you can create amazingly innovative looks.

Texture has become more important than pattern in the decorator's lexicon now that neutrals and creams are so popular, particularly in apartments and townhouses. A neutral scheme can look

1

downright dull and boring if it's not handled properly. So when you are working with neutrals, remember that textured surfaces throw strong shadows that give dimension and visual interest.

### TRICKS OF THE EYE

A room is better balanced when there is a combination of pattern and texture. You can play up the good features of a room and disguise (or at least minimise) those which are less attractive by being clever with pattern, such as painting stripes or using a check or floral fabric to upholster the walls.

Disparate features, such as walls at odd angles, sloping ceilings or walls which are marked or damaged, will be unified by pattern, camouflaged by a textured paint finish or completely covered up by fabric. But note that strong food smells cling to fabric so this wall treatment is not suitable for dining rooms.

### A GUIDE FOR SUCCESS

The key to success with both pattern and texture is careful planning and much experimenting with sample boards.

With pattern, it's the scale and size you have to worry about. With texture, try to avoid too many similar textures in a space. A polished smooth gloss finish against a rough stucco rendered wall is infinitely more exciting than textures of the same kind. You might have similar colours for walls throughout a series of rooms, but by varying the textures from matt to rough they'll reflect light in a different way and, consequently, look different, creating a more interesting effect.

Some textures lessen the intensity of a colour. If you want to use a strong colour all the way around a room, but feel it may be overpowering, paint effects can be your best ally. Sponging or ragging or random brushing in a suede or sand finish will tone down the look of a strong colour.

### 1. STORAGE AS ART

Putting the wall to good use is justification for building in excellent storage. Creating a great piece of design is another thing altogether. This wall takes on the guise of artwork. Behind the stunning blackbutt timber grid is a whole wall of cupboards and drawers, with the television taking centre stage.

### 2. LINE A KID'S ROOM

Children really do love a personalised environment. Here, stripes are all the go. Using masking tape to create smooth edges as she worked, a clever mum has handpainted wide stripes in gold and amber, with contrasting antique white used for the ceiling and trims. .

### 3. TILE TEXTURES

The beauty of tiles is that you can find one to replicate the look of just about any natural stone. Practically speaking, ceramic tiles score high for durability and they bring an interesting finish to a room. When combined with other textures, they literally jump in your face with style. In this bathroom, the rustic painted finish and tiles complement each other not only in colour but also in texture.

### 4. PAD A BEDROOM

Covering walls with fabric is one of the oldest of all decorative devices. As well as its unique capacity for camouflage, fabric improves sound insulation, which makes it especially good for bedrooms. This domestic sleeping spot has the mood of a five-star hotel, with its wonderful feature wall of separate panels padded and upholstered in a chic cotton damask. But avoid using fabric on walls touched with damp; it will encourage mildew.

2 3

4

## THE NEW PAINT FINISHES

**COLOUR WASH** gives a weathered look to a wall by using two colours in two coats. You can apply the topcoat with a dry brush in random or crisscross directions, or dab it on with a moist paint pad.

**DISTEMPER** has a traditional powdery finish – apply it with a roller or brush.

**EGGSHELL FINISH** gives a subtle lustre. Apply two coats with a roller or brush.

**IMPASTO** looks like plaster. Paint the second coat in a random crisscross.

**METAL EFFECTS** gives a soft metallic look. Brush, roll or spray it on.

**PEARL FINISH** has a subtle shimmer. On the second coat, do a crisscross action with a 100mm (or wider) brush.

**SAND WASH** has a light texture. Roll on two coats with vertical strokes.

**STONE EFFECT** gives the worn look of stone. Paint with a crisscross action on the second coat.

**SUEDE EFFECT** has the look and feel of brushed suede. On the first coat, use a long nap roller; on the second, paint with a wide brush in a random crisscross.

# OPEN THE DOORS

DOORS TODAY ARE MORE ABOUT CONNECTING SPACES THAN CLOSING THEM OFF. AS WELL AS BEING AN ENTRY, THEY ALSO FRAME THE VIEW FROM ONE SPACE TO ANOTHER, GIVING YOU THE OPPORTUNITY TO COMPOSE A SCENE.

### 1. LIFT, DON'T SEPARATE

An industrial edge suits apartments in warehouse conversions, and this garage-style, steel-framed door has plenty of grunt. The door's lifting action doesn't impinge on the interior space, allowing the living area to fully embrace the courtyard. A conventional glazed door provides an alternative means of access. The projecting balcony above provides shade.

### 2. USE A PIVOT POINT

Fitted with a panel of clear glass, this large pivoting door offers enticing glimpses of the home's riverside setting. It's part of a scheme of bifold doors, clerestory windows and timber shutters that makes the most of the natural light and breezes. North Queensland silky oak frames the door, providing a connection to the shutters and bifold doors.

Living spaces that have a light, breezy quality, a sense of openness and a close connection with the great outdoors are almost an obsession among modern Australians. Increasingly, gardens and courtyards are treated as an extra room of the house, with the indoor and outdoor spaces designed as one, particularly when it comes to what's laid on the floor and the colour palette used.

Along with big windows, glazed walls, skylights and glass atriums, doors – or, more accurately, walls of doors – are key elements in designs that achieve those feelings of openness and light.

Open-plan additions and banks of glazed doors, which in some cases extend across the width of the house, are turning previously dark period homes into light-filled dwellings. Houses that make use of cross-breezes for natural ventilation and harness the sunshine for winter warmth are also energy-efficient.

Modern manufacturing methods allow for larger glass panels to be used as doors, while steel can be fashioned into frames much thinner than those of aluminium or timber, allowing for minimal visual intrusion and a more industrial look. Timber frames, however, tend to be more appropriate for older-style houses.

## TYPES OF DOORS

Whether doors are folding, pivoting, sliding, lifting or conventionally hinged will affect how 'open' a room feels. French doors are the time-honoured way of connecting a house to its courtyard or garden, and as such are suited to more traditional-style homes. Being a hinged door, they require space for swinging open, and their grids of square glass panels have an obvious impact on the view.

Sliding doors are more space-efficient, but the size of the opening is limited by the fixed panes required for the doors to bank against or the cavity space into which they recess.

Folding doors, with the doors neatly stacked to the side, provide generous, unobstructed openings, although the folding action requires some clearance and the doors can be temperamental to operate. When closed, the doors segment a view into a series of vertical lines, with a degree of boldness that depends on the width of the frame and its finish.

Pivoting doors rotate around an offset column instead of using hinges. The door's opening and closing action has an attractive floating quality that marries well with sparse, contemporary interiors. For a space with an industrial aesthetic, a garage-style lifting door can create an uncompromising sense of openness.

## GOING WITH THE FLOW

More than ever, doors are about opening up rather than closing off spaces. Sliding doors between rooms increasingly serve as movable walls, helping create a greater connection between the rooms for more flexible and space-conscious living. Glass doors with translucent or opaque finishes allow for the passage of light to a home's interior while preserving privacy. But increasingly, we are doing away with conventional internal doors altogether, as living spaces become more free-flowing and open plan.

2

### 1. MATCH THE LOOK

The correct style of door – and most importantly, a suitably proportioned design – is integral in maintaining a period look. In this century-old terrace house, the bedroom's original french doors were in good condition. Painted in a flat charcoal colour, they gain contemporary flair while still harmonising with the facade.

### 2. PLAYING A TRICK

A doorway as a secret passage brings a theatrical quality to this period-style room. The visual trickery of the trompe l'oeil bookcase relies on the real one to the far right. Such a door treatment is only suitable for accessing a room that is rarely used or serves a private function, in this case a bathroom. The ledge of the lowest shelf serves as a handle.

### 3. TRANSLATE THE JAPANESE SCREEN

The use of screening found in traditional Japanese interiors translates well to modern East-West styles of decorating, where clean lines, natural materials and contrasts of light and dark predominant. For this over-sized sliding door, translucent glass panels framed in walnut-stained oak joinery mimic shoji ricepaper screens and allow a generous spill of light while safeguarding privacy. A bulkhead hides the tracking mechanism and the floor is left free of a runner.

### 4. FOLD-AWAY STYLE

Finished in white and fitted with shutters, these bifold doors take on a definite French air in an apartment full of Gallic touches. Doors fold outwards, so as not to impinge on the bedroom's floor space, and stack flush against the flanking walls to create a generous opening to the balcony. The doors' classic design makes a suitable frame for glimpses of the terracotta-paved courtyard with its parterre-style plantings.

### 5. A SLIDING DOOR FOR ADAPTABILITY

Extra-wide sliding doors serve as movable walls, giving flexibility to a tight floor plan. This 2.3-metre wide, full-height sliding panel can close off a library-cum-guest room or open the space to become an extension of the living area. The panel slides into a wall cavity to save on valuable floor space, and a ceiling-hung mechanism leaves the floor free of tracking. Panels of opaque glass in an American white-oak frame allow through light.

### 6. RESPECT TRADITION

Period-style houses can still meet modern needs for airy spaces while remaining true to their decorative spirit. In this coastal home, inspired by the traditional whalers' cottages of America's Cape Cod, classical french doors are full-height and glazed to draw in natural light and embrace the views. Antique brass door fittings and a tasselled key provide the appropriate decorative detail.

### 7. MAKING DOORS A GRAPHIC FEATURE

Doors should either make their presence felt or be entirely inconspicuous, rather than being somewhere in between. These American cherrywood veneer cupboard doors and charcoal-painted timber balcony doors provide visual punch against plain white walls. Mesh panels for the cupboard doors create a breezeway effect to aid ventilation and add to the country aesthetic. The door to the bathroom blends with the walls to avoid being a detail.

4 5

6

7

1

## CHOOSING DOOR HARDWARE

Replacing door furniture is a simple way to revitalise an interior. Take cues from the period of the home. Colonial, Federation, Art Deco – each has a distinctive look when it comes to door furniture. Contemporary interiors offer scope for different designs, although linear architectural forms tend to predominate, and this should be reflected in the choice of hardware.

Interesting handles can make a plain door more distinctive, but where the door itself is a feature, hardware should be chosen for its subtlety.

Door hardware should complement the design and finish of other fittings in the room, such as light fittings, wall brackets and ceiling fans.

Keep the design and finish consistent from front door to cupboard doors, with just a change in scale. Alternatively, use a different set of hardware on a separate floor – perhaps one with softer lines and less robust finishes on the private level, which gets less wear and tear.

Fit in with the design of the door. Don't use straight handles on a door with rounded panels, for example, and use hardware in proportion to the door's size. With the rise of more monumental entries, handles are increasingly elongated.

For ease of use, it helps to have some degree of colour contrast between the door and the handle – perhaps polished chrome on a dark door and satin chrome or satin stainless steel for a light-coloured door.

With front doors getting a bolder look, embracing everything from sleek metal finishes in pewter, nickel or zinc to pivoting sheets of slumped glass or ornately carved antique temple doors, the choice of appropriate door hardware is demanding even greater consideration.

Good quality door hardware really is worth the expense, so remember to allocate it an appropriate amount in your building budget.

2

### 1. OPENING BIFOLDS

Floor-to-ceiling bifold doors stack neatly away to seamlessly merge interior and exterior spaces. Here they span the width of the house, aiding ventilation and drawing in light as well as connecting the living room to the deck to form one large room. Joinery in Syrian cedar matches the shutters used elsewhere in the house and adds to the architectural impact of the doors. When closed, the bifolds' run of bold vertical lines exaggerates the height of the ceiling, adding to the sense of airiness.

### 2. A BOLD FRONT

Big doors inevitably make more of an entrance. Research even suggests that the more impressive the front door, the greater the perceived value of a house. As a focal point, front doors can justifiably make a splash. This full-height pivoting door takes its design cue from local weatherboard cottages. Constructed of western red cedar shiplap boards, oiled for a modern flat finish, it matches the cladding on the upper facade of this home. An elongated stainless steel handle accentuates the linear look of the timber.

### 1. ROMAN DRESS

Roman blinds are more formal than roller blinds. They're composed of flat horizontal folds of fabric which pull up into a series of wide pleats; when let down, they hang loose against the window. They were especially popular in England during the 18th century and are just as at ease in contemporary interiors. Here, roman blinds hung individually over the casements address the need for light control in a north-facing bedroom. The blinds are made from a heavy cream cotton edged with bullion fringing.

### 2. SHADE A FRENCH DOOR

A soft semi-sheer cotton is perfect for dressing french doors. The doors can be tricky to screen because they have to be able to open without interference. Narrow roller blinds which follow the lines of the glazing and simple, straight curtains hung each side of the doors are good. But you could also try an inverted pleat blind like this one, which is less rigid than a roman blind and can be hung about 10-15cm in from the doorframe.

# WHAT WINDOWS WEAR

WINDOWS WERE ONCE SEEN ONLY AS PART OF THE EXTERIOR OF A HOUSE, HOWEVER NOW THERE'S MORE EMPHASIS ON THEIR ROLE IN BRINGING THE OUTDOORS IN – ESPECIALLY IN ROOMS THAT LACK DIRECT ACCESS TO A GARDEN. BUT BIGGER ISN'T ALWAYS BETTER WITH WINDOWS – HOW YOU DRESS THEM IS.

Colonial architecture turned a blind eye to the environment, fortifying domestic homes against the elements with thick walls and tiny windows that were rarely oriented to maximise the sun, and almost always ignored the view outside. Today, the architectural vernacular takes a different approach, bringing us closer to the outdoors, however great or small.

## THE BIG PICTURE

If you are building a new house or renovating an old one, don't incorporate big picture windows without any sense of composition or rhythm. Having vast window walls in a home rather than individual windows is a wonderful ploy to harness light, but it presents little opportunity to use curtains or blinds. Without such window dressings, an interior can look aggressively bare.

Increasing the glass content of a room means you increase the amount of sunlight and, therefore, the amount of heat coming in. Conversely, glass (which is not a good insulator) also permits more heat to escape during winter. The solution is blinds and curtains; they are great tools for controlling light and glare in summer and heat loss in winter, and also let you turn the outdoor view on and off, or somewhere in between.

2

## THE LOWDOWN ON GLASS

Windows have been glazed only since the 15th century. At first, glass could only be produced in small sizes, so these were put together in the style of leadlight to create a window of reasonable size. In 1959, British manufacturer Pilkington invented float glass, which resulted in glass of a uniform thickness, brightness and clarity. The types of glass available for modern windows, panels and screens are excitingly varied:

**TOUGHENED** glass (tempered glass) is safety glass.

**LAMINATED** glass has a transparent layer of plastic sandwiched between two sheets of glass, which are bonded together under pressure. It's generally considered safer than toughened glass, but is more expensive.

**WIRED** glass has a fine steel mesh sandwiched between two separate layers of glass. It's used where there is the need for increased security or fire-resistance.

**FLOAT** glass is perfectly flat and can be manufactured in a variety of thicknesses to suit different applications.

**TINTED** glass has a small amount of metal oxide added to the molten mix. Tinting increases the amount of heat absorbed by the glass, so that less penetrates through to the room.

**LOW-EMISSIVITY** (low-E) glass allows maximum daylight into a room but retains the heat at night, acting as insulation.

**DECORATIVE/TEXTURED** glass has a relief pattern made either by casting or by pressing a design onto the semi-molten surface with a roller. This texture decreases transparency.

**ETCHED/SANDBLASTED** glass is also known as frosted glass. It's been surface-treated by sandblasting or acid-etching and has a matt look which obscures views and diffuses light.

**COLOURED** glass can look like traditional stained glass or have a painted coating.

**GLASS BLOCKS** come in clear, frosted, satin and textured and coloured finishes. They're a stronger, more secure infill for a window opening and are good for blocking heat and noise.

### 1. BREAK UP GLARE

A multi-paned window wall is a strong architectural feature. By breaking up the expanse of glass with timber battens, there is less glare than with full-height glazing.

### 2. PRIVATE VENETIANS

Venetian blinds are ideal for bathrooms: they can be adjusted to control the amount of light and fresh air and provide total privacy. In this bathroom, cedar blinds are a strong design element.

### 3. STAYING BARE

If you have beautifully designed windows and no privacy problem, then think about not covering them at all. This living room has a view to a secluded courtyard and enjoys complete privacy and filtered sunshine. Here, dressing windows is unnecessary.

### 4. CHOOSING LOUVRES

Louvred wooden shutters are perfect for letting air and light into a room. Wide louvre blades (90mm) give a less obstructed view and greater air flow, while the narrower blades (60mm) work well in small spaces or where a view is negligible.

If the view from your window takes in a number of disparate elements rather than a panoramic vista, you might be better off with a series of identical windows, side by side. This will bring more natural light into the room, and offer 'snapshots' of the outdoors.

A similar effect can be achieved using a single large window with vertical and horizontal crossbars in a grid formation (colonial bars).

## WINDOW STYLES

While many late Victorian terraces are blessed with perfectly proportioned, full-length windows and french doors, most other traditional house styles in Australia feature proportionally small casement or multi-paned windows (think leadlight, coloured and etched glass). Many styles open out (hopper) or up (awning), and some are fitted into a bay.

However windows have got progressively bigger as our domestic architecture has changed to embrace natural light and use more open floor plans.

## WINDOW DRESSING

Despite a decade of the stark realism of bare windows, the curtain has returned to flatter and soften a room. However, furbelows, flounces and overly ornate finishes have been run out of town and what is most popular today is sheer, floaty fabric hung in single layers on simple rods. It's often used in tandem with blinds for better light control. Blinds, too, have gained status – they are becoming the new feature walls.

Whatever you choose to dress your windows with will be determined by the style of room and by the window itself. The more architectural your windows and doors, the more structured your window

dressings should be. A window should wear something that accents its best feature – whether it's a deep casement or a beautiful arch. But the treatment could also be used to disguise a poor frame, irregular shape or even cracked glass.

A pelmet, deep frill or swag placed above a window, so that its bottom just disguises the top of the glass, is a clever way to lengthen the look of a too-short window. Or you can bring a large window into a more intimate scale by swooshing a swag of fabric over its curtain pole.

Traditionalists tend to see windows as opportunities to drape, swag, trim and tassel. But contemporary decorators will say that since we live in the 21st century and don't wear 19th-century clothes, our windows should reflect our lifestyles and be dressed in fabrics that share the same spirit and sense of simplicity seen in the current fashions.

### 1. DRESSING ARCHES

Arched windows require lateral thinking to effectively screen sunlight and give privacy. Shutters are an ideal solution; they become part of the architecture rather than merely decoration. In this bathroom, wide plantation shutters are fitted for privacy on the lower part of the window. The elegant curved section above gives the impression of a fanlight and remains uncovered to let in natural light.

### 2. A CHIC SHEER

Today's sheer voiles and muslins do much the same job as the net curtains of decades past – they diffuse light and protect privacy. But they have a sophistication that makes them very much a thing of the 21st century. This exquisitely embroidered muslin drapes and gathers well, adding a romantic touch to a bedroom window.

### 3. TRADITIONAL TOILE

Toile is a refined cotton or linen print whose intricately detailed patterns depict rustic farm or family life. The popular toile de Jouy was made in France in the 18th century and was usually printed on a white or off-white background in monotone red, blue, green or black. The fabric design of these simple side drapes has a similar look to toile and introduces a touch of country charm to a family room. A coordinating gingham check cotton features in the tie-back and decorative cushion.

### 4. FILTER THE LIGHT

If you want a soft, non-intrusive blind, go for a roman shade made with thin dowel and a semi-sheer or textured fabric which will allow light to filter through when the blind is let down. Fix the blind above the architrave so that when it's completely pulled up, maximum light can enter the room. This blind has the interesting effect of stripes, but is in fact pieced fabric edged in black cotton.

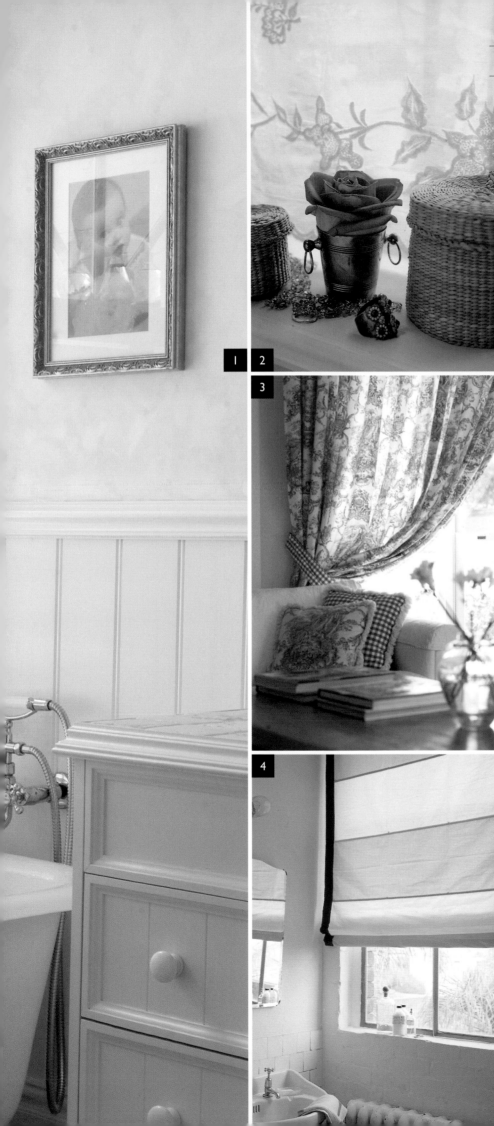

## BLINDS, SHUTTERS OR CURTAINS?

Decide what you want the window covering to do. Does it need to block out sunlight and heat? Is it for privacy, or is it to draw attention to the shape of the window, or even disguise an ugly view?

• If you want to detract from irregularly matched or boring windows, try roman blinds and avoid loud printed fabrics.

• To capitalise on the view, choose a simple window treatment such as sheer drapes or sunscreen blinds.

• For a less-is-more treatment, go for a roller blind, but if you love a tailored look, try roman blinds.

• If your inner-city home is starved of light but you need privacy, curtains of sheer and translucent fabrics are ideal.

• For absolute light control, choose venetian blinds or plantation shutters.

• To completely block out both the heat and light, choose plantation shutters, coated curtains or lined blinds.

• If you love how the light streams through and makes shadow patterns on the walls, then choose a woven bamboo, grassweave or oriental-style blind.

## WHAT FABRICS GO WHERE?

When it comes to curtains, the first rule is to never skimp on fabric and never compromise on fabric quality. Select a cloth suited to the job you want it to do. **PURE SILK** is made of a protein, so it's sensitive to ultraviolet light in a similar way that your skin is damaged by the sun. Silk curtains wear better away from sunny

### 1. USE ENOUGH FABRIC

Stingy-looking curtains will never make the grade. The first thing to remember is be generous with your fabric: at least double the width of the window and then some. Most curtain-makers prefer plain, natural fabrics because they hold their shape, but this beautiful sueded fabric is a perfect match for this chic room. Secured on rings and a wooden rod, the simple drape can be pushed aside to allow easy access to the garden.

### 2. TOTALLY EXPOSED

In this converted studio, the beauty and originality of the steel-framed windows is the feature of the room, so covering them would be a negative. To prevent your furnishings fading rapidly from the unscreened daylight, pull them away from the windows. Remember, too, you need darkness for sleep. It's best to keep your exposed spaces for living.

### 3. MODERN SCREENING

When minimalism became fashionable, shutters and blinds took over from curtains. And while less structured curtains have returned to favour, the sunscreen blind is often still the first choice of designers wanting a clean-lined look. Stainless-steel supporting columns project from the window wall in this contemporary dining space which is shaded with white 'e-screen' blinds.

### 4. MAKE A FRAME

A plain box pelmet suits the scale of this elegant bedroom. Single, unlined drapes are neatly pulled back with tasselled silk cord to frame the window.

rooms, and deteriorate more quickly than man-made or blended fabrics.

**SILK TAFFETA** has a crisp, brittle finish and drapes well. It is suitable to use for full-length curtains.

**LIGHTWEIGHT NATURAL FIBRE** fabrics such as muslin, voile and linen are ideal for tab-top curtains. Sheer muslin can be hung behind curtains to give privacy during the day – great in casual spaces.

**COTTON CALICO** was originally used as a curtain lining, but now is popular for all styles of window treatments.

**PRINTED LINEN** drapes well and suits all kinds of window dressings.

**JACQUARD AND TAPESTRY** fabrics are rich in texture and pattern – ideal to use for heavy curtains or blinds.

**HEAVY WOVEN COTTON** is quite robust. Use it for unlined curtains and blinds.

**DAMASK** drapes elegantly and works well for curtains in more formal spaces.

**VELVET** is a luxurious fabric that is most suitable for full-length lined curtains.

**GATHERED CURTAINS** can be used in bay windows, tall wide windows and where there is little room above the window for a curtain pole.

**SINGLE CURTAINS** can be simple panels, and suit both tall and short windows.

**A PELMET AND FULL-LENGTH CURTAINS** are suitable for tall windows which are longer than they are wide. Strategically placed, pelmets can also be used to make a window look taller.

**DOUBLE CURTAINS** allow you to layer the colour and texture of different fabrics – perfect for living rooms and bedrooms.

**PLEATED BLINDS** look their best on narrow windows – choose a fabric which doesn't easily crease.

**TEXTURED, RATTAN AND BAMBOO BLINDS** allow light to stream through and make shadow patterns on the walls.

2

3 4

## THE HARD FACTS ON HARDWARE

**It's the clever details which put the 'wow' factor in window treatments.**
**CURTAIN POLES** have come into their own now. You are spoiled for choice – from painted and stained wood, to polished chrome, wrought iron and Perspex. But for followers of minimalist style, simple stainless-steel wire with fittings from a ship chandler is preferred.
**FINIALS** are ornaments fitted onto each end of the pole, which stop the curtain rings falling off. This is where the opportunity to be creative comes in. A finial may be a beaten metal or crystal ball, a carved wooden disc, or a Perspex spear, a gilt leaf or a jewel flower.
**ATTACHMENTS** such as curtain rings in wood, iron, stainless steel or brass are common. You can also attach a curtain to a pole with twisted wire, clips, tabs, fabric ties or rope and eyelets.
**SUPPORTS** that you choose for your curtains will affect their look. You can use a pole or a curtain track (which should be concealed). Some styles of blind can be hung from a rod if they have a rod pocket, but most are hung from a lath attached to the wall with brackets.

**HEADING** is a tape which is sewn onto the top of the curtain to control the way it hangs. If you want it gathered, or if you want box or pencil pleats, there is a heading to assist.
**TIE-BACKS** are a curtain's signature – they hold back a curtain or hold up a blind.
**TRIMMINGS** such as feathers, crystal droplets, ribbons, braids and beads give a haute couture look to curtains and blinds when sewn into the design or fashioned into a tie-back or tassel.

# TAKE THE FLOOR

WHAT'S UNDER YOUR FEET HAS A BIG EFFECT ON THE LOOK OF A ROOM. THE FLOOR CONSTITUTES A BIG SWEEP OF COLOUR AND IS AS IMPORTANT AS THE HUES ON THE WALLS IN DEFINING AN INTERIOR STYLE. CHOOSING ITS FINISH SHOULD BE ONE OF YOUR FIRST DECORATING DECISIONS.

By the size of their surface area alone, floors inevitably exert a major influence over the style and character of a room. They are likely to consume a large chunk of any renovation or building budget and, as such, will need to maintain their looks and appeal well beyond the short term. What material you choose for the floor comes down to practicality as much as appearance and comfort – of all the surfaces within the home, floors must be the most capable of taking the rough and tumble of everyday living.

How you surface your floor will dictate its overall impact within a space, allowing it to shout its presence or simply serve as a quiet, neutral backdrop. However, as a general rule, a floor should always be darker than a ceiling. If you're after a look that can ride the fickleness of fashion trends and adapt to evolving decorating schemes, opt for neutral-toned flooring materials. A room's colour and detail can always be provided by rugs and other home furnishings.

Laying the same flooring throughout a home creates a sense of spaciousness,

cohesion and flow. Alternatively, a mix of flooring materials can be contrasted to define the different functional zones in a space. The transition may be as subtle as a change in the floor's texture rather than colour or tone. Patterned flooring is best reserved for sparsely furnished areas of the home, such as hallways, where there are fewer competing elements.

Naturally, any area that is subject to heavy foot traffic, such as hallways or living rooms, will need flooring that is tough and durable. Where a living area connects directly to an outdoor space, consider using tiles, concrete or stone, which can be laid across both to visually draw them together.

While both kitchens and bathrooms need a floor that's non-slip and easy to clean, a kitchen floor should also be able to take the knocks and stand up to spills. Bathrooms should be water-resistant and have that barefoot appeal without being slippery when wet.

In all cases, choose the best quality material you can afford, and ensure it is expertly installed and well maintained.

**1. BLENDING OLD AND NEW**
The points of transition between different flooring materials need careful consideration if they're to avoid giving you a visual jolt. An abrupt junction between the deep red of the original jarrah floor of the hallway and the pale Victorian ash parquetry used in the rear addition has been avoided here by a clever blending of the two timbers. The parquetry adds a contemporary lightness, enhanced by its simple patterning.

### 1. A LIMEWASH LOOK

A limewashed timber floor complements the soft, white-on-white look of this French provincial-style interior. Floorboards can be coated with a diluted paint solution or rubbed with a lime paste, with the effect of toning down the brash orange tones of certain timbers while allowing the grain and general warmth of the wood to show through. The matt sealer used here produces a soft, chalky finish.

### 2. DURABLE SATIN

Tallowwood has exceptional durability and makes for a floor that is versatile and easy to work with, thanks to its uniform grain and absence of gum lines. While high shines on floors have tended to give way to more natural-looking matt and satin finishes, durability has been the trade-off. The toughness of a finish declines as the proportion of matting agents increases. A satin finish, like the one used here, is a good compromise.

### 3. GO FOR CONTRAST

Jarrah's rich colour is a great foil for an all-white space, although it can be too dark and dominating for a large area that doesn't receive much light. The jarrah floorboards of this bright white kitchen relate to the timber of the front deck, with a subtle change in texture from a polished to an oiled finish.

### 4. USING TERRAZZO

Terrazzo, a flooring often associated with Italian interiors, can lend a masculine quality to a space. Laid as tiles or poured as a topping, it comprises an aggregate of granite, marble and glass chippings mixed with concrete to give a broad range of patterns, textures and colours. This polished concrete floor takes on the look of terrazzo with an aggregate that picks up the colours of the interior finishes.

## BAMBOO FLOORING

A relative newcomer to the flooring market, bamboo offers a greener alternative to hardwood boards. Actually a grass, bamboo is a sustainable and renewable resource with strong environmental credentials. Just as important, its blond good looks marry well with the contemporary love of spare, light-filled spaces.

While timber-like in appearance, bamboo has superior strength, stability and moisture resistance to most timber species. And as the majority of Australian hardwood floors tend towards darker shades, its pale colouring makes it very useful for achieving a lighter look without sacrificing strength and durability.

Bamboo flooring is supplied as laminated tongue-and-groove boards, which can be laid by sticking them down to a suitable subfloor or by using secret nailing to attach them to joists and bearers.

The boards can be pre-finished in a high gloss or a matt finish, or they can be supplied raw for finishing with any product, including wood stains, that you would normally use on timber.

2

3

### 1. PARQUETRY FOR A RICH EFFECT

Parquetry floors are composed of strips of hardwood laid into geometric patterns, which often suggest the direction of movement within a space. They have a complexity and richness that goes well in hallways and large formal spaces. This distressed tallowwood parquetry floor assumes the mellow patina of age, bringing a 'tailored' European feel to a series of salon-style rooms.

### 2. TAMING THE KNOTS

Cypress pine floors are associated with Australian houses built in the 1950s and 1960s, but are often too highly figured and bright for modern tastes. Applying a coat of limewash is one method of knocking back the orange tones and grain. But here, brilliant white walls and cabinetry in a kitchen flooded with natural light serve a similar purpose; their laid-back tones produce a quietening effect on the timber's colour and complexity.

### 3. MAKING A MIX

A mix of flooring materials in a soothing natural palette adds subtle detail to this luxurious coast-inspired bathroom. The pebbled border creates a slip-proof area around the spa, while a narrow band of charcoal grey mosaics articulate a slight change in floor level. Soft blue-grey mosaics with colour-matched grout provide a non-slip transition to the bedroom's high-gloss floor tiles without a jarring shift of colour.

## 1. STAINS FOR DISGUISE

Staining preserves something of the integrity of timber by adding colour without masking the grain. Many of the dark tropical hardwoods associated with traditional-style interiors are now on the endangered list, so staining can produce a similar effect with alternative timber. This new floor of messmate has been given a polished dark walnut finish that complements the sophisticated air of this Colonial-style interior.

### 2. LAY A PATTERN

These blush-toned ceramic tiles were the starting point of an interior inspired by the French country look. The laying pattern, emphasised by dark grouting lines, defines the different functional zones within the open living space, with tiles set on the diagonal to visually push out the walls. Unlike glazed tiles, grout can be porous, causing it to darken over the years as it absorbs grime and stains.

### 3. A COOL GLOSS

The classic combination of black and white brings a crisp, balanced tone to a clean, contemporary space. The polished finish of the vinyl floor tiles reflects rather than absorbs the light, and 'cools' the expanse of black. For a space that receives heavy foot traffic, commercial grade vinyl takes the knocks and provides comfort underfoot.

### 4. FAKE A STONE LOOK

Modern ceramic tiles can re-create the look of stone at a fraction of the price of the real thing and without its physical weight and sealing requirements. Glazed or vitrified tiles are as durable as stone, too, and are ideal for high-traffic areas such as living rooms. These porcelain tiles have a textured, non-slip finish and an uneven edge to resemble stone flags. Their neutral tone reflects light and provides a subtle backdrop for eclectic furnishings.

### 5. SUBTLE LIMESTONE

A floor's large surface means its colour and texture can dramatically affect the light within a room. Here, the pale even tone of a honed limestone floor lends a natural glow and measured calm to this modern living space. Limestone is a favourite in contemporary interiors. It can be plain or flecked and has a range of colours, from creamy white and beige through to grey-green and almost black.

## CONCRETE FLOORING

A cost-effective alternative to laying tiles or stone, polished concrete floors are immensely tough, durable and easy to care for.

Floors are laid as a slab or can be poured as a screed over an existing concrete slab. Colour, texture and pattern can be provided by using pigments, paints, stains and coloured aggregates.

Concrete may be fashioned to imitate any number of stone types, or its surface detailed using paints, stains or even coloured chalk. Timber or metal strips, tiles or stones can be embedded within the floor, or a top layer of self-levelling resin can be applied to produce a sophisticated polish similar to colour-backed glass.

Aggregates in a concrete mix are exposed by grinding back the floor surface, which is then smoothed and polished for a refined finish.

As concrete is porous, the surface must be sealed. Waxing and oiling can create a finish with richness and warmth, or a polyurethane lacquer may be used for a matt, satin or high-gloss finish.

### 1. REFINED CONCRETE

Polished concrete floors can look refined without compromising their raw integrity. Concrete's monolithic surface marries well with the minimalist look of this contemporary space. Slow curing ensured the surface of this raw concrete floor was free from cracks, and meticulous wet and dry polishing produced its smooth, lustrous finish.

### 2. FAUX FLAGSTONES

Concrete provides the perfect blank canvas for creative expressions of colour and texture. This faux flagstone effect was produced for a French provincial-style interior and its courtyard after real stone was ruled out because of its thickness. Grout lines were cut into the newly laid concrete slab and the surface painted to resemble aged stone. A waxed finish lends a natural honed effect and the grout lines were filled for authenticity.

### 3. DIY EFFECTS

Transforming a standard concrete slab into a beautifully patinated floor doesn't have to cost the earth. Here, the mottled effect derives from soil and other building materials trodden into the slab's surface during the construction process, which coloured the concrete with natural earth pigments. The surface was then sealed and coated in polyurethane with a semi-gloss finish.

### 4. TERRACOTTA TOUCHES

The warm earthiness of a terracotta floor immediately evokes thoughts of relaxed Mediterranean-style interiors. Terracotta colours vary according to the character of the clay, from the peachy orange of Mexican tiles to the rich reds of Burgundy in France. When made by hand, terracotta tiles have a roughness and irregularity that adds to their rustic appeal. The suede-like surface of these unglazed, machine-made terracotta tiles makes a pleasing contrast to the white gloss finish of the bathroom fittings.

### 5. A SEAMLESS EFFECT

Seamless matt or satin finishes create a calm, contemplative mood. They also have a warmth about them that is lost with highly polished surfaces, which tend to appear 'busy' and cold. These vitrified porcelain tiles mimic the look of honed limestone, bringing a soothing quality and barefoot appeal to this luxurious bathroom. Machine cut and rectified (butted up), the tiles produce a seamless finish that reads as a single slab.

5

### 1. SWEEP SHOT

A grand, sweeping staircase with handrails and treads of polished kauri pine is the central focus of this spacious entrance foyer. The stairs lead from the front door up to the main living area, with its peaked ceilings and elegant Georgian-style arched windows. Moving down the stairs to the front door gives the owner a thrill every time.

### 2. DESIGN OF THE TIMES

Designed in 1960, this staircase retains a modern edge with its stainless-steel supports and glass balusters. The stairs feature timber treads which are covered in non-slip black-studded rubber, safely secured with aluminium stripping. The space beneath the stairs is a quiet, light-filled spot for relaxing on Scandinavian woven-webbing chairs.

# STEPPING UP IN THE WORLD

IN THE DECORATING PROCESS, IT'S SOMETIMES EASY TO LOSE SIGHT OF THE SPACES WHICH CONNECT YOUR ROOMS TO EACH OTHER. THE STAIRCASE IS ONE OF THE HARDEST-WORKING OF THESE AREAS AND, TREATED PROPERLY, IT CAN ALSO BE A POTENT FOCAL POINT IN THE DESIGN OF YOUR HOME.

Staircases are generally overworked and overlooked, yet they are an important element in establishing the architectural logic of the home. As well as providing physical access to all levels of a house, they give visitors their influential first impression of you and how you live. In a design sense, a staircase can introduce strong vertical and diagonal lines or gentle, graceful curves, and create rhythm, pattern and sculptural forms.

### STAIRWAY TO HEAVEN

There are many different staircases: they may be straight, quarter-turn, dog-leg, circular or spiral, using either landings or winders (see Glossary on page 46) to create the changes in direction.

A straight stair stretches from lower to upper level in one flight. It's probably the easiest to build but it needs quite a lot of space and fitting it into a floor plan can be difficult. A dog-leg stair reverses flights a full 180 degrees at a landing, while a quarter-turn stair makes a 90-degree turn using either a landing or winders. A circular stair generally sweeps upward in a broad curve, and a spiral stair twists around a central pole.

For the sake of safety, building standards give a suggested number of risers in each flight, and the steepest allowable angle. They also govern the maximum riser height and the minimum tread size, the

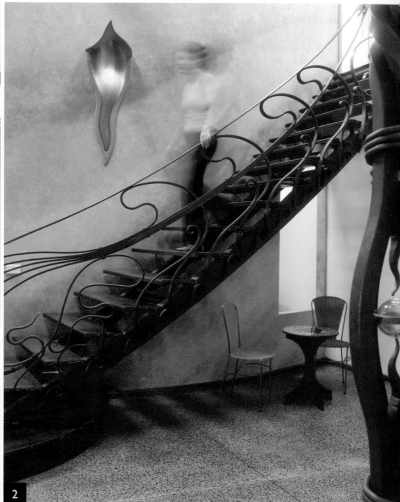

## 1. BALANCING HUES

In a tri-level penthouse, timber stairs highlighted by deep blue walls are the core of the traffic flow. Finding the right feature colour to play up the rich honey tones of a timber staircase was easy. Wood is a warm colour, so its opposite is a cool blue – a perfect contrast, a perfect match and a perfect balance.

## 2. ART ON THE RAIL

Turning a staircase into a work of art requires some creative effort with the style of the handrail and balustrade. In this home, a sweeping curved balustrade has been fashioned from wrought iron.

## 3. KEEPING IT STRONG

A steel and timber staircase brings a sharply sculptural element to a house. Its working-class background – think factory floor and ship's gangway – puts it in good stead to withstand the rigours of a busy household. It has been made into a striking feature by being 'boxed' in with floor-to-ceiling slatted cedar screens.

## 4. TEST YOUR METAL

Inspired by the minimalist elements of warehouse design, a metal staircase should be used in context with its surroundings. This dramatic staircase slices through the living area of a converted warehouse. The iron for the treads was left outside to rust before being sealed. The balustrade is made of steel.

## 5. GO DOWN BELOW

Mimicking the proportions of a turn-of-the-century terrace, this modern townhouse has under-stair storage for a fridge and a small bathroom hidden behind a set of cedar-framed sliding glass doors.

headroom over the stairs and the height and width between handrails.

How you move between levels in a home is important, and the staircase affects the way a new area is introduced. In older, more traditional homes, when a new storey is added the staircase often starts in the hallway. Here, it's best to keep the style sympathetic.

## STYLE COUNTS

Victorian or Edwardian-style staircases look very solid and are built of timber with decorative newel posts and ornate banisters. The steps are usually covered with carpet or a runner, and the space beneath the stairs becomes a valuable storage area. Runners can sometimes make stairs look narrower than they actually are, so if it's the illusion of space that you're after, consider painting or completely carpeting the treads.

When the staircase is positioned in a contemporary, architect-designed house or extension, it can become something of a big 'statement' piece. Stairs which lead to communal living rooms can be more open and inviting than those which lead to private areas of the house.

Stairs with open risers have quite a lightweight feeling, allowing glimpses through to other parts of the house. Handrails and banisters can be highly ornate, fashioned from timber, steel or wrought iron. On the other hand, barely-there banisters made of glass or fine stainless-steel wire – or no handrail at all – will give a sense of translucency. This throws the staircase itself into relief, making the steps appear like a sculpture. It's a style popular in minimalist decor, but is not suitable in a home where there are young children.

Traditional Mediterranean stairs often have ceramic tile treads which introduce a pattern on the steps.

Open, metal treads look great in converted warehouses and contemporary interiors as they reduce the visual bulk of a stairway, but they can be just as noisy

to live with as an uncarpeted wooden staircase. Fixing embossed rubber to the steel treads will ensure safe footing and minimise the echo.

## CHANGING VIEW

You can make your stairs work in other ways. For example, a large landing with chairs and a small table can be a place of interaction. Make it the 'communication centre' where you put your keys, mail or leave messages for other family members. Wider than normal steps at the base of the staircase could provide a place to sit.

**UNDERCOVER ACTION**

**Use the dead space under the stairs by:**

- Turning it into a neat home office.
- Building in storage for bulky utility items such as the vacuum cleaner and brooms.
- Making it the designated spot for sports gear such as golf clubs, tennis racquets and skis.
- Building in a dry goods pantry or a spot for the fridge.
- Making it a place for the washing machine and dryer.
- Installing hooks for hanging wet-weather gear or the kids' hats.
- Using it to display favourite collectables and family photos.
- Building in open shelves for books and magazines.
- Placing a comfy couch there to create a private 'me' space.

## STAIRCASE GLOSSARY

**BANISTERS/BALUSTERS:** the uprights supporting the handrail.

**BALUSTRADE:** the handrail and row of balusters that support it.

**FLIGHT:** a consecutive series of stairs.

**NEWEL:** the principal post at the end of a flight of stairs.

**TREADS:** the horizontal surface of the steps in a staircase.

**NOSING:** the overhanging edge of the stair tread.

**RISER:** the vertical surface between the top and bottom of the stair's treads.

**WINDER:** a tread that is wider at one end than the other for a gradual change in direction of the staircase.

### 1. GREAT FOR A DISPLAY

A traditional dog-leg or U-shaped staircase works well in an entry hall and is often better positioned away from living areas. This shape has the advantage of avoiding a single straight flight of stairs, which would impose on valuable room space. The deep alcove it creates below is a great place to display a signature piece of furniture like a favourite cabinet. Here, the owner has positioned a baby grand in what appears to be a made-to-measure spot.

### 2. SPACE SAVER

High ceilings and an emphasis on space led to the creation of these sweeping stairs. The flow of the living area remains uninterrupted by the curved staircase off to the side. The stairs are shaped around a Japanese-inspired column featuring kwila timber, complementing the timber steps and handrails.

You can change the view as you climb the stairs by using the adjoining expanse of wall as a gallery or display area for family photos. Resist the temptation to echo the line of the stairs by hanging your pictures in a stepped formation. Arrange them instead in several separate groups spaced out along the length of the stairway. Or you can hang a large artwork, painting, quilt or rug on the double-height wall – these items need space around them to look their best and it's rare to have a room with that much unbroken wall space.

### THE UPS AND DOWNS

For safety's sake, careful consideration must be given to the covering or finish of the stair treads; you'll also need to have good, firm handholds.

Highly polished timber treads look beautiful but can be dangerously slippery – avoid them at all costs. Also ensure your stairway is well lit and never leave shoes, toys or other items on the stairs – they are an accident waiting to happen.

Staircases must be lit so that you can easily distinguish between the risers and the treads. The very worst type of light for stairs is flat and shadowless.

Wall lights which are positioned to follow the progress of the treads and downward directed lights on stair landings are the most effective option for stairway lighting. Having on-off switches located on both levels is another essential. Spotlights give a blinding glare when seen from certain angles as you walk up and down steps, so forget about using them near stairways.

**3. STRAIGHT UP**

A long hallway provides the space needed for a straight stairway. Treads and risers in honey-toned Victorian ash give the impression of the stairway being precisely folded against a stark white wall. Its lack of a handrail would pose a safety problem for small children.

1 | 2

# HOME FIRES

THE FIREPLACE CAN STILL BE THE FOCAL POINT OF A MODERN INTERIOR. ITS FLICKER BREATHES LIFE INTO A SPACE AND SATISFIES A PRIMAL NEED TO GATHER AROUND A COMFORTING SOURCE OF WARMTH AND LIGHT.

Although ducted heating and reverse-cycle air-conditioning have removed the practical need for a fireplace, many of us still hanker for a hearth at home.

## NEW-GENERATION FIRES

While nothing beats the all-round sensory appeal of a real log fire, the look and feel of the latest ceramic-log gas fires make them a convincing as well as a convenient and efficient alternative.

Rather than needing a chimney, modern gas fires directly vent through the wall, so are easier to position. Modern electrical fires are vent-free so they overcome the usual difficulties of including fireplaces in apartments. The best of the electrical designs offer a realism close to a gas fire.

Freestanding fireplaces are perfect for open-plan living spaces. They serve a large area but will also create a sense of intimacy by allowing people to gather around in much the same way as a camp fire. However these fireplaces are inclined towards the massive scale to suit the generous proportions of these spaces.

A transparent, two-way fireplace can be shared between neighbouring rooms or installed on an exterior wall to serve both indoors and out. Rear-ducting has encouraged the placement of fireplaces against an external glazed wall, allowing views all around without the distraction of a vertical flue. For greater impact, fireplaces are being raised above floor level.

In minimalist interiors, a fireplace is often little more than a hole in the wall. A simple trim, typically in black, stainless steel or stone, stands in place of a mantel or surround. Existing fireplaces are often painted to blend with the walls to simplify the look for a contemporary space.

### 1. REVIVE AN OLD FLAME

A period fireplace becomes a pivotal feature in a space of clean lines and contemporary furnishings. All but the chimney section of a wall was demolished to create an open-plan living area. Mouldings were added for more impact and the fireplace was painted to blend into the pared-back space. A simple mirror and restrained ornaments keep things razor-sharp modern.

### 2. FIRE AGAINST GLASS

Having rear-ducting allows this gas fireplace to sit comfortably against a wall of glass, with no vertical flue to disturb the view or the room's sense of airiness. The fire surround is in white, adding to the lightness of touch in this casual living space.

### 3. CENTRAL STATION

With its soaring chimney breast, a central fireplace reflects the generous scale of this country retreat and creates a divide between the different living zones. Deliberately sculptural and imposing, the chimney's expanse of white is relieved by an offset display niche. A wrought-iron tool set and woven baskets to store firewood emphasise the relaxed, country look of the house.

1

2

## STORING WOOD

Traditionally a fireplace was located close to an external door for easy access to the woodpile, with a small supply of fuel stored under the cover of a porch. To store a fireside supply of logs, sturdy baskets are great in a rustic-style space. Wrought-iron holders, from simple racks and 'baskets' to elaborate sets with fire tools, come in many styles, from period to contemporary.

For a minimalist interior, built-in storage is best as it keeps the floor free of clutter. One approach is to raise the fireplace above floor level to create space for a wood box underneath. Alternatively, alcoves can be built within the fireplace wall or in joinery alongside. Artfully arranged, a log-filled niche can look as good as an abstract painting.

### 1. KEEP IT DISCREET

A hole-in-the-wall gas fireplace with simple black trim offers minimal visual distraction from a display of artworks. By being raised slightly off the floor, the fireplace assumes greater importance within the space without being overbearing. A pair of abstract paintings on each side of the fire provides a decorative focus for the fireside sitting area.

### 2. SLOW COMBUSTION

For a bush property with access to a steady supply of firewood – and plenty of room for its storage – a slow-combustion heater is the design of choice. With an old leather sofa placed nearby, it forms the heart of a cosy sitting area close to the back door, and is perfect for warming hands and feet when coming in from the cold.

### 3. A GREAT DIVIDE

For 20th-century American architect Frank Lloyd Wright, a rough-hewn fireplace was often the starting point for his house designs. Here, a stacked slate fireplace anchors a living room while concealing the kitchen behind. The slate gets a modern edge with a stainless-steel flue.

### 4. SCALE IT RIGHT

A classic marble fire surround and cast-iron fireplace can be equally at ease in a modern scheme, providing their proportions match the scale of the room. This salvaged ensemble occupies the site of the original fireplace, with the surround raised slightly to align with the skirting board.

### 5. UP THE IMPACT

Recessing a fireplace in a gyprock wall and painting the breast has given this hearth impact. This fireplace originally stood proud of the wall; it was dwarfed by windows on either side before the addition of an enclosing wall balanced the proportions. The adjacent wood box fills a redundant space.

### 6. GO TWO WAYS

A two-way fireplace lets a dining room and games room share a single fire and gives a light-filled view when it's not in use. A rough sandstone surround gives the fireplace gravitas.

3 4

5 6

Today's bathroom is metamorphosing into a pleasure palace. Just as attention has been given to 'designer' bathware and surfaces in this bathroom, so too has necessary storage been added with a creatively critical eye.

Once you have chosen finishes for the walls and doors, and decided on the style of windows in your home, it's time to look at those other essential items. There's the mass of storage that a modern family must have, the careful positioning of artificial lights and the manipulation of natural sunlight. The modern home must also take into serious account today's fast-moving technology, wiring itself for everything from the internet to remote-control home theatre.

### 1. A CASUAL STACK

A mix of storage styles can look rather lovely in a traditional bathroom, alluding to the charm of a Bed & Breakfast. If you keep linen and spare towels in the bathroom, it's essential to have excellent ventilation, otherwise moisture will make the linen damp and the towels smell musty. Here, a step-stool provides the ideal spot for fresh towels and bath requisites.

### 2. SLEEK BUILT-INS

You can never have enough storage in a bedroom, but if you can't have a walk-in wardrobe, opt for built-ins instead. The main bedroom in this older-style apartment has been turned into a slick, contemporary space. Storage units finished in a high-gloss polyurethane fit between structural columns.

# PUT IT INTO STORAGE

THE PRINCIPLE BEHIND GOOD STORAGE IS TO HAVE MORE THAN YOU THINK YOU NEED – CLUTTER MULTIPLIES AS FAMILIES GET BIGGER. GREAT DESIGN IS AS IMPORTANT AS FUNCTION, AND ANY STORAGE SHOULD FIT IN WITH YOUR HOME'S DECORATIVE STYLE. DEVISE A MASTER PLAN FOR STORAGE THAT INCLUDES EVERY ROOM IN THE HOUSE.

Storage is all about order. And nothing puts order back into the smooth running of a household faster than good storage. It doesn't even have to be clever, just so long as it's realistic.

Weighing up the house in its entirety, rather than room by room, means things can be stored more logically. For instance, it's easier to pull your kids' sports gear from a cupboard in the hall than to keep it in an already cluttered bedroom.

Before you begin to take stock of your storage needs, look around you. Whether you live in an established home or have recently built or renovated your place,

you may discover a whole pile of things collected over the years that have become irrelevant to how you live.

There may be a stash of gadgets you never use, instruction manuals and spare parts for appliances and whitegoods which have given up the ghost or which you have long since upgraded, gifts you can't use and clothes that don't fit, child-rearing books and, worse, books that you know you aren't ever going to read again.

Make a promise to yourself to toss the lot before you begin seriously editing and subtracting your possessions. Don't waste precious space by storing junk.

### 1. SHELVE A GALLERY

Pigeonhole shelving running the breadth of a bedroom is a fresh take on the traditional cupboard and shelf option. An artist displays her collection of art glass in this off-white shelving unit, turning her bedroom into a gallery.

### 2. KID-STYLE STORAGE

Kids' rooms need a thoughtful approach. There always has to be a place for masterpieces created by the youngsters, so storage units should be built so as not to compromise on wall space. Perfect in this situation is a pair of narrow, beech veneer, floor-to-ceiling cupboards fitted with shelves. Underneath the bed are three big roll-out drawers/boxes on castors – great for toys.

1

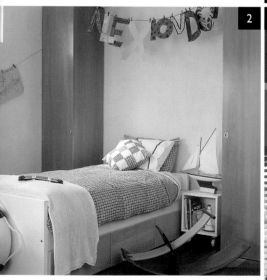

2

3

### 3. DRAWER THEM IN

Children of every age need easy-access storage, preferably at floor level. Encourage them to be tidy by providing plenty of deep drawers that shoes, toys and games can be hurled into. Here a divan bed, with drawers underneath and cupboards at each end, was designed to integrate with the desk and maximise the space of this small room.

## WHAT DO YOU NEED?

Determine how you live to decide what kind of storage you need. If you are someone who cringes at the sight of the day's newspaper left crumpled on the floor or clothes or books strewn all over the sofa, then you will be living in pain unless you provide a wide variety of storage options to relieve the pressure.

You may be energised by simplicity, where every surface and table top are not weighted down with family belongings. On the other hand, you may relish clutter, be comforted by it and need possessions around you, within reach. Or you could be a disciple of minimalism, gleaning satisfaction from being free of the weight of ownership. Finding a home for books and accessories will never be a problem for you because you choose not to buy them in the first place.

Possessions and belongings constitute a very real part of what gives many of us pleasure in our homes; if you are a dedicated clutter-puss sharing life with a fanatical minimalist, then opting to keep everything well regimented and hidden behind the closed doors of wall-to-wall built-ins will deny you any real visual satisfaction. It's better to choose an open and shut case – a mix of closed and open storage to give both partners pleasure.

## TYPES OF STORAGE

Order is simply a way of arranging things so they can be accessed in the most efficient way. You can hang them (from racks, rails or hooks), contain them (in drawers, cupboards, boxes and baskets), stow them (under beds, on top of cupboards or in trolleys) or shelve them. The idea is to streamline your belongings as much as possible, with storage being conceived as part of the overall look of a room and designed to fit what is being stored.

## 4. FAMILY CONTAINERS

A family room is usually on the go 24/7, and efficient storage is the backbone of its successful operation. Newspapers, books and magazines, games and toys, electronic gear, craft items, kids' writing stuff … all must be found a place. The best option here is sturdy baskets, such as these woven fibre ones, or lidded plastic crates and pull-out drawers.

## 5. CUSTOMISED CHIC

Built-in storage can be tailored to suit your possessions, and allows for more creative options than the conventional bookcases either side of the fireplace. Here, the architect has designed American walnut-lined display units in concert with a dramatic painted panel. The curved bulkhead gives a sense of drama.

## CAREFULLY CLOSETED

**These clever tips will help you keep control of your wardrobe, rather than your wardrobe controlling you.**

- Put nothing on the floor.
- Hang garments just above your eye level.
- Have rails to hang shirts and skirts in a double deck.
- Include large pigeonholes for folded T-shirts and shorts, etc.
- Make all shelves adjustable.
- Include shelving for shoes beneath short items, or in a vertical cabinet.
- Install pull-outs wherever possible for easy access.
- Use good-quality plastic hangers. If you don't want your clothes creased, always pad your hangers.
- If you can't see into your wardrobe, what's the use? Install a light inside the cupboard.
- Hang all your clothing far enough apart so that it airs properly and doesn't come out crunched up.
- Colour-code your closet for easy selection. Group blacks, whites, darks, brights and neutrals.
- Before you build a wardrobe, establish the maximum reach for deep drawers. That way you won't lose things down the back.
- If you have lots of clothes, use tie racks and shoe holders to help keep things tidy.
- Keep in mind that a woman's wardrobe is always bigger than a man's – so allow for it.

### I. CLOTHES CONTROL

In this walk-in dressing room, compartments have been carefully allocated and clothing sorted by colour; her clothes to the left, his to the right.

### 2. IN THE HALL

Older-style houses always had a hall closet and it worked, so try to include a cupboard somewhere near the front door for keeping hats, school bags and sports gear. Install hooks for hanging wet-weather gear. In this home, everything has a place in the entrance, with a bench for drying wet shoes.

### 3. STARRING SHOES

Being the owner of a large collection always poses the problem of storage. This owner has a shoe collection to rival Imelda Marcos, so she built an entire wall of shelves for them.

## BUILT-IN

This is usually considered closed storage. Customised floor-to-ceiling or wall-to-wall cupboards are an investment which pays great dividends. They maximise space, giving tailor-made integrated storage for just about anything and everything. You can store bulky items like kids' toys, disguise television, audio and computer gear behind cupboard doors, stack books and magazines, stow out-of-season clothes and so on.

While a built-in cuts into a room's size, it also helps streamline the look – particularly if it's painted the same colour as the walls – and is the ideal storage solution for apartments and small-space living.

## FREE-FORM AND FREESTANDING

The average family accumulates a huge amount of stuff, but organising things by type, rather than owner, can help. Individual storage solutions work best here. The more you can compartmentalise storage the better. Use old suitcases, big baskets, plastic crates on wheels and decorative storage boxes. Make access easier with trolleys and cupboard units on castors, shelves fitted with pull-out baskets, and cabinets with sliding drawers and racks. Remember, too, that traditional furniture like a French armoire, Chinese wedding chest, blanket box, tallboy, lowboy or chest of drawers are big on personality and add immense character to a space as well as being practical.

## SHELVING

This open storage is suitable for every room in the house, but if you worry about dust, moths, cooking grease and fading from sunlight, then store your precious articles under cover or behind closed doors.

Today there are incredible shelving units so beautifully designed they are artworks in themselves. They put to the

test the rule that shelves should be seen, but not before the objects they hold.

The most mundane objects take on a life of their own when well grouped. Ideally, shelves should be only wide enough to display one layer of objects, but of course this never happens — especially in a kitchen.

No matter what, kids love shelves — make them secure so littlies don't pull them down if they try to climb up them.

## STORAGE ROOMS

If you are a control freak, one of the best ways to keep tabs on your stuff and keep your life in order is to have a stowing place like a walk-in dressing room, a pantry in the kitchen, a library-cum-home office or even a section of the

garage. And children will benefit from having their toys and play equipment stored in plastic crates and boxes on open shelves in another room designated as a playroom. This leaves their bedroom floor free from the daily detritus.

## SHOW AND TELL

Including some open shelves and niches in the design of your built-ins gives you a place to display your collections, photos, artworks and anything else that takes pride of place in your house.

Freestanding cupboards and drawers, however, allow you a few more decorating options. As well as hiding the good, the bad and the ugly, they give interest and variety to a plain wall with their shapes, handles or knobs.

### 1. THE BOOK STACK

If you want an alternative to traditional bookshelves, search the second-hand shops. An unusual freestanding stacking unit obtained by the owner of this cottage becomes a focal point and provides instant access to her books.

### 2. EVERYDAY DISPLAY

There's potential for storage as display in almost all kitchens — imagine the organisation evident in the pots, utensils, crockery and condiments which are pulled out of cupboards with monotonous regularity. The open shelving above this island bench is a boon to the cook as it provides a display space for often-used items and favourite pieces of pottery.

### 3. ON DOUBLE-DUTY

Multi-function storage suits today's lifestyles. In this country kitchen, a big chunky bench made from recycled timbers and fitted with industrial castors extends the food preparation area, as well as offering a place for wine and serving platters.

3

## STORING DISKS AND TAPES

**The first thing to remember is to keep disks where they're needed: software near the computer, CDs near the hi-fi and videos and DVDs near the TV.**
Any storage system works best if fitted with containers which will hold smaller items safely. Drawers in units or on castors, shelves, alcove cupboards, bookcase-style units sized to hold CDs or tapes, and freestanding units, like CD towers, are all possible solutions. Metal strip dividers and plastic trays are an affordable, practical solution for organising videos, DVDs and CDs in purpose-built drawers. Once in place, they're permanent and sturdy.

One of the simplest things to remember with disks and videos is to avoid stacking them too high or too deep on shelves. If you have to reposition the entire stack every time you play some music, you'll never put the cases back again properly. Remember:

- It doesn't matter whether you keep the disk in its original case or another sleeve, so long as it's kept clean.
- Always keep your collection away from direct sunlight.
- Avoid heat or humidity.
- Store upright, not flat.

4

### 1. GOING LOW-LINE

Built-ins tend to monopolise wall space so if you want to visually expand a room, opt for low-line cabinets with translucent doors. This modern sideboard goes one better with a mirror hung above to give the illusion of a window. Being on castors makes it easy to move to anywhere in the room; it would make a great divider between living and dining spaces.

### 2. SNOOZE ABOVE

It's important for teenagers to have both privacy and a place to study. When space is limited – such as in a townhouse or apartment – you have to be flexible. To make double use of this compact space, the bed was positioned on top of the desk and the deep steps up to it are fitted with drawers. It's fun and there's loads of storage for a teenager, as well as a spacious desk.

### 3. FAMILY SIZED

Large families need storage big-time to make rooms cosy and comfortable. Kids need baskets and boxes while adults prefer something less in-your-face. Here, seamless storage units wrap around the spacious living room, providing display for a collection of family photos, keepsakes and favourite books. The watermelon-coloured fabric used for the slipcovers and as lining for the shelves is a clever design move.

### 4. CLOSE AT HAND

Keeping things behind closed doors is one solution to the problem of order in the kitchen. But in this renovated space, an island bench opposite the family dining area offers a place for organised display on open shelves. Finished in wenge wood, the shelves are ideal for keeping dining condiments, cups and saucers and even recipe books close to the action.

### ARE YOU A MINIMALIST?

Do you have zero tolerance for clutter? If you prefer very little on display, then discreet storage – like built-ins – is for you. Storage which appears seamless and an integral part of the architecture will be especially appealing.

Shelves built around a door or within a niche or recess in the wall (even a window seat or a storage box), will read to the minimalist as a structural element, not an afterthought. Pure minimalists will want no handles or embellishment on doors, with the cupboards finished so they 'vanish' into the walls.

### OR DO YOU LIKE A MIX?

Most of us would prefer to live with a mix of closed and open storage, built-ins and freestanding cupboards. In a family home this combination gives a better balance. Children need to see what goes where, and they won't be encouraged to stash and stow if they can't work out how to do it.

### 1. AN ORNAMENT

Decoration and function can combine wonderfully in a light. This egg-shaped lamp is beautiful, whether it's on or off. The original egg lamp is the Uovo, designed in the early 1970s by architect Gae Aulenti and the technical department of Italian company Fontana Arte. The Uovo sits on a metal ring that keeps airflow in the glass, making it possible to fit higher wattage lamps. The egg lamp shown here pays homage to Aulenti's iconic design, but lacks the metal base.

# THE INNER GLOW

LIGHT ITSELF IS AN ESSENTIAL PART OF A HOME'S DECOR, ILLUMINATING WORK ZONES AND SCULPTING SPACES TO PLEASE THE EYE.

The modern design mantra may be to bring in fresh air and sunlight, but this does little for a home's night attire. How you manipulate artificial light has a big impact on how your home looks and how well it functions. It's time to farewell that solitary pendant swinging in the centre of every room; lighting schemes now play with light and shade to bring an almost sculptural look to a room.

There are three categories of lighting: general, which provides a room with its overall lighting; task, which focuses extra light on work and reading areas; and accent lighting, where a spotlight or downlight is used to target and bring attention to a particular feature.

Halogen downlights can be used as accent lights, to provide even background light, or as wall washers for a decorative effect – it depends on the beam spread of the bulb. Incandescent spotlights can bounce their beam off walls for a softer illumination, while uplighters make a play of light and shade against feature walls. Fluorescents still hold their own for task lighting, but they can also be concealed in a cove around the perimeter of a ceiling for an intriguing effect.

Lighting is being developed that allows you to carry the same design theme from indoors to out. There are light cubes that double as side tables, and table and standard lamps that sit just as comfortably in the living room as out by the pool. And those cane Hawaiian flares have had their day – new-look flares with stainless-steel bases are decidedly more swish.

### 2. SHADE CHIC

Paper shades over a pair of pendant lights deliver designer cool to this stairwell. Repeating a shape in a different scale is a trick often used by graphic designers and these oblong shades are reflected again in a mirrored panel. It's a stylish way to illuminate a traffic zone and lift it above the purely practical. Low-voltage downlights in gimbal fittings provide good, even background lighting elsewhere but, during the day, sunshine comes for free through a large skylight.

**2** **3**

**4**

## 1. KEEP IT MELLOW

Bedroom lighting should be soothing. A pair of wall lights flank an uplighter to provide subtle illumination over this bed. Bouncing their glow off a freestanding wall painted in purple (behind is a walk-in wardrobe), the trio of lights gives the room a much sexier edge than a standard, central pendant fitting. There are light switches above both bedside tables, making it easy for either occupant to flick the switch. Dimmers dial down the glow for a mellow mood.

## 2. A CLASSIC LOOK

Light fittings are an important part of a decorating scheme. These shaded sconces suit the elaborate style of a Venetian mirror and give the finishing touch to the entire setting. Placing lights on each side of a mirror is kinder on your reflection, too, as the even light means there is no shadowing to play up every line in your face.

## 3. READING RIGHT

A pair of Tolomeo lamps by Artemide are more commonly spotted on desks, but here are perfect as bedside lamps. The opaque shades throw light downwards, not outwards, and the anglepoise stands allow them to focus light on a book, not on a sleeping companion's face. In this little nook, they can also act as accent lighting, bringing attention to an ornate shade and lotus print.

## 4. ADAPT OLD FOR NEW

A classical sensibility directs the lighting in this genteel scheme. The glass shade hanging above the French oak table originally held candles, but has been adapted to take incandescent candle-shaped bulbs. Adding drama and a sense of occasion to the room is a large painting which is highlighted with a spotlight.

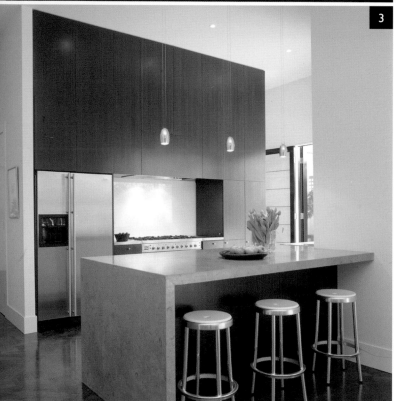

### 1. A DINER'S SPECIAL

In dining areas, you'll want a soft light that's flattering to both food and faces. Incandescent bulbs are better suited to this than fluorescents, which may have a pink or green cast. A classic tiered fitting with incandescent candle bulbs sits well with this period-inspired decor and brings an attractive, warm light to the dining area. A series of table lamps, wired to turn on with one switch, gives a gentler illumination than overhead fittings, especially when it's diffused through fabric shades.

### 2. KEEP IN THE PINK

There's a touch of pink behind this bathroom mirror – an unexpected patch of colour in a neutral scheme. As well as looking good, this slip of warming red counteracts any bleaching effect from the light bouncing off the pale walls. Having true-to-life skin tones reflected in a mirror is a big bonus when you're putting on make-up. Fluorescents are best for this sort of close work, as they don't put out heat. Choose a good triphosphor type to avoid looking washed out.

### 3. STRIKE A BALANCE

A kitchen needs good task lighting for work areas but a softer effect around dining zones. In this kitchen, sunshine streams through a glass door during the day and downlights provide general lighting at night. The wide bench has a trio of halogen pendants above. At full strength they work as task lighting; when dimmed they're perfect for dining by. Reflective surfaces bounce light around the room, so a little goes a long way.

### 4. ADAPTABILITY

Bathroom nirvana is having an adaptable scheme with sunlight, good task lighting around the mirror, and an option to dim the main bulbs for a night-time soak. But don't overdo wattages around reflective surfaces or the room will be sizzling, not serene. In this room, a shot of sunshine through a skylight makes it a much happier spot to greet the day. Recessed shelving is accented with a downlight that helps break up the visual block of a timber veneered wall.

4

### 1. UP THE WATTAGE

Halogen spots emit a focused, white light and deliver the oomph needed to illuminate this dark-toned cellar dining room. A white surface reflects 80 per cent of the light that hits it, but darker colours and matt surfaces absorb light, and need more wattage for adequate light levels.

### 2. ON THE SPOT

Accent lighting puts the focus on a particular feature in a room. This home is also an art gallery and has spotlights picking out a 17th-century Japanese wall panel and a collection of vases. They can be moved to focus on different pieces when the display changes. Halogen trapeze lighting serves for general illumination. Remember, too, that reflectors in halogen downlight fittings produce a precise beam of light. As lamps are available in different beam spreads, changing the effect from general illumination to pinspots of light is as simple as swapping bulbs.

### 3. GET CRYSTALS CLEAR

There's been a rebirth of things pretty, and chandeliers now make a shimmer in both traditional and contemporary homes. To keep those crystals sparkly, you'll have to clean the chandelier once a year. The best way is to make a diagram of where the crystals go, then disassemble the drops and wash them in hot water with a mild detergent. When you return the hanging pieces to the fixture, work from the inside to the outside, giving each piece a quick polish as you go.

## WHAT LIGHT WHERE?

**INCANDESCENT TUNGSTEN BULBS** put out a warm-looking light and can be dimmed. They go well in living areas, bedrooms and even bathrooms. Drawbacks are poor energy efficiency and a short lifespan (1000 hours).

**HALOGENS** produce an intense white light that's good for colour rendering. They last up to 5000 hours, but run hotter than tungstens and need heatproof mountings and dichroic reflectors. Low-voltage bulbs require a transformer.

Depending on the bulbs' beam spread, halogens can work as background lighting, task lighting, as an accent light for artworks, or as wall washers. A network of halogens gives good even light for kitchens and bathrooms, but they can also be dimmed for a different ambience. In living areas, a downlight grid can easily overlight the space, so fit them with 20- or 35-watt bulbs rather than 50-watt ones.

**FLUORESCENTS** come as straight or doughnut tubes, or as long-life bulbs. They produce a haze of light rather than a beam (so there's less shadowing) and don't emit heat, so are good for desk lamps. They go well in rooms where ambience isn't the main concern: kitchens, bathrooms and workshops. They can't be used with standard dimmers.

# THE HI-TECH REVOLUTION

A MODERN HOME CAN BE WIRED FOR SOUND, LIGHT AND AIR, WITH ITS OWN HOME THEATRE AND BROADBAND INTERNET LINK. WHAT WILL TOMORROW BRING?

Advances in technology are making homes increasingly 'intelligent'. Through home networks, you are able to integrate systems such as lighting, security, audio and video for touch-button control, or link devices to sensors and clocks for energy-saving efficiency.

You can press a keypad as you walk in to trigger a 'welcome home' mode that turns on the air-conditioning and lights, de-activates alarms and pipes sweet music through your multi-room audio system.

Technology is also revolutionising the scope for entertainment and education within the home. With DVD, digital, cable and satellite television and a host of internet-based services, you can tune in to an ever-expanding smorgasbord of audio-visual media from your living room.

Big screens, surround sound and razor-sharp imaging are re-creating all the sensations of the cinema experience in a corner of the lounge or, if you have the space, a dedicated home theatre room.

Televisions can be used for much more than just 'watching the box' – they can serve as game platforms, computer monitors and home cinema screens, with modes for displaying surveillance from security cameras, or even be art in disguise. Then there's the evolution of more interactive forms of television.

Home offices, too, have become a ubiquitous part of modern life, with computers and peripherals linked on networks that imitate those used in the commercial workplace.

But enjoying a hi-tech home does not have to be at the cost of living in a minimalist space or a more traditional interior. Making all this technology invisible relies to a great extent on hiding the cabling and wires, preferably along wall and roof cavities and under floors.

The best time to install a wiring system is in the early stages of building or during a major renovation of an existing home, when it's possible to access walls. An alternative to hard-wiring, however, is wireless LAN (local area network), an emerging technology that uses radio frequencies instead of wires.

**1. COCOONING**
A custom-built wall unit, finished in matt white polyurethane and framed in beech veneer, brings a light touch to the big screen, which is also housed in white. Sliding pocket doors keep the area in front free from clutter, with storage underneath and to the left of the television for stowing appliances, CDs and DVDs. A bar fridge is built into the end of the unit, adding to the comforts of cocooning in front of the box.

1  2

### HIGH-SPEED CABLING

Cabling is hardly sexy, but the right choice of cable will help 'future-proof' your home as technology develops.

Wiring networks based on high-speed CAT 5 (or even CAT 6) data cable and RG6 coaxial cables are better than conventional copper wiring. These cables facilitate faster, more reliable data transfer, and when forming a structured network, are linked to a central control hub which acts as the brains of any home control system. Press a remote-control somewhere in the house and this sends a signal to the central hub, which then activates the relevant devices. In some configurations, a PC can control the system, operating through a broadband internet connection.

You should decide at your home's planning stage which rooms will have access to TV, video, audio, telephone and internet, and where outlets, keypads, wall-mounted televisions and speakers need to be installed. By planning the furniture layout at this early stage, down to the size and placement of sofas and tables and lamps, you will also pinpoint the best location for wall- and floor-mounted power points. This will allow for seamless integration, without cables and sockets on view.

Offering considerably higher rates of data transfer to CAT 5 are fibre-optic cables and the associated laser technology, but these come with a hefty price tag. Used for networks in the commercial sector, fibre optics are slowly infiltrating into the home market, but only at the luxury end of the scale.

### EXISTING WIRING

Trying to retro-fit a structured wiring system into an existing home is highly impractical. But there are options for setting up a connected home other than slicing through finished walls and having cables trailing across floors. Simple adaptors allow your home's existing electrical wiring to double-function as a network, carrying power and data simultaneously. This requires no new cables and can be accessed in any room that has a standard wall socket.

### WIRELESS

Wireless networking, like power-line networks, requires no additional cabling and offers flexibility of access. But its physical range is limited and it can be quite tricky to set up. Based on radio technology, signals pass through walls but can slow down noticeably where dense materials, such as masonry or concrete, are involved. There are various options for going wireless, including WiFi (wireless fidelity), Home RF and Blue Tooth. As wireless networks are vulnerable to hacking, it's important to configure them for security.

It's possible to use more than one technology for setting up networks, for example using a power-line network to

## NETWORKING

- Where you've more than one PC, you should consider linking them up to a computer network. This allows you to share peripherals such as printers and scanners, plus internet access, and have the ability to take part in multi-player games.

- If you're suffering from slow internet response over a modem dial-up connection, move to broadband. This is essentially a high-speed, constant internet connection that allows high volumes of data to be downloaded at considerably faster speeds. It also allows more than one networked computer to access the internet at the same time.

- Broadband can be delivered via cable (which uses pay-TV infrastructure), satellite (generally slow and costly) or the existing telephone wires (ADSL). Although piggybacking on the telephone wire, ADSL doesn't take over a phone line itself, allowing both to function at the same time.

- Broadband also opens up a world of IP (internet protocol) control of the home. This uses the internet and the home network to communicate with electronic appliances and systems such as security, lighting and so on. Get ready for appliances with internet connection capabilities, which have the brains to contact the provider should they need a service.

3

4

### 1. MINIMISE CLUTTER

A stack of 'black boxes' can make less of a fuss in a black and white interior, for obvious reasons. Here, a large television on a freestanding unit appears to meld seamlessly into the glossy black floor. With space at a premium, the owners chose a television that incorporated both a DVD player and VCR in the one unit. A stereo, speakers and aerial are stowed in a cupboard fitted with the necessary sockets. A sculptural CD rack is positioned to distract from the cabling.

### 2. LISTENING IN

Sound was given serious consideration in this chill-out space within the living area. As cabling for the speakers, television and video couldn't be run through the walls, it has been integrated into the custom-built joinery. The speakers are fronted in grey mesh for a more subtle effect. Seating is arranged to fully benefit from the stereo sound.

### 3. A PUBLIC COMPUTER

Kids in this home surf the Net and do their homework in a spot between the kitchen and living area, allowing for casual supervision. The desk breaks the mould of traditional office styling, allowing it to sit comfortably within the public space. The computer is networked to the main home-office computer downstairs. Computer storage on castors blends with the adjacent modular storage, while black tubing conceals the cabling.

### 4. GO INTO RECESS

A recess for audio-visual equipment can often be included within a fireplace wall, especially as modern slim-line televisions require a space of minimal depth. The doors of this cupboard, which houses the television, VCR and DVD player, slide back into the recess for minimal intrusion on the floorspace.

reach any dead spots in a wireless connection, or expanding an existing cabled network with wireless technology to connect an extra computer in an upstairs bedroom.

## SHOW OR STOW

The TV has swelled in size, but most other appliances have got smaller. Shelf sound systems and hi-fi components are increasingly compact. Those audio 'black boxes' now also come in white or silver for a more stylish look. But regardless of individual styling, racks of equipment are likely to clutter a space and are best stowed behind doors in custom-built cabinets that mirror the finishes and lines of joinery elsewhere in a room. These cabinets should be vented to allow air to circulate and heat to disperse.

## TELEVISION

The television was once a bulky black box that sat in a corner and compromised many a decorating scheme. Slim, flat-screened sets of plasma and LCD (liquid crystal display) have changed our view of the box. They can be mounted flush on the wall, offering greater flexibility for their placement.

Although the trend is towards bigger screens, plasma, which comes in larger screen sizes than LCD, delivers the wide-screen format at a depth of less than 10cm. A popular place to hang or recess a plasma screen is above a fireplace, in lieu of a painting, although the appliance should not be exposed to excessive heat.

Big screens have found appropriate settings in the large, open-plan living spaces typical of modern homes. When it comes to size, front- and rear-projection systems are in a league of their own. But remember, big televisions can easily overwhelm smaller rooms.

Also take into account your viewing position. As a rule of thumb, seating should be positioned at a distance of between five to eight times the screen height of your television. For open-plan spaces where a television may be viewed from different zones, an LCD television or plasma screen offers a broader viewing angle without a deterioration in picture quality. Alternatively, mounting the set on a recessed bracket allows the screen to be angled for better viewing.

How much light there is in the room will also dictate your choice of television. Flat screens tolerate a reasonable amount of glare, but front- and rear-projection systems work best in a dark room, with heavy curtaining on windows. For this reason – but also because of their sheer size and the need to mount or lower a projector from the ceiling – front-projection displays are best reserved for dedicated home theatre rooms.

The conventional cathode ray tube (CRT) television still provides the widest range of options, including flat-screen and wide-screen formats and models

3  4

### 1. THEATRE STARS

A dedicated home theatre room allows for the greatest synergy between technology and interior design. Smart wiring lets televisions and speakers in rooms throughout the home access the DVD player, pay-TV channels, VCR and hi-fi, thereby saving on equipment and space. The home cinema system can also be linked to a laptop for projecting digital images of family happy-snaps on the wide screen. This integrated scheme has speakers recessed into the wall and painted to match, while the rest of the electronic components are stored inside a custom-built walnut cabinet on the wall facing the screen. Well-padded seating offers the requisite comfort and, along with the carpet and heavy drapes, enhances the acoustics of the space.

### 2. BLACK BACKING

Painting the screen wall a dark colour creates maximum viewing impact and has the effect of drawing you into the picture. In this dedicated home cinema, with its tiered arrangement of 18 recliner chairs, the full theatrical experience is conjured by painting the space black. The main screen is flanked by two smaller screens to allow viewing of three sporting events simultaneously.

### 3. A LITTLE BIT TRAD

Big screens and black boxes can be jarring additions to a traditional-style interior. Here, audio-visual appliances have been confined to a dedicated home theatre in the basement. The classic theme is continued with chesterfield-style leather seating, plush fabrics and the mahogany-stained joinery, which displays books and conceals audio-visual equipment. Walls are upholstered for acoustic value and to maintain the masculine, clubby look of the space. The centre speaker of the surround sound system is built into the storage unit that runs under the screen.

### 4. PLASMA PLUS

With its ritzy European styling, this media room gives hi-tech the tailored look. The plasma screen was selected to fit the scale of the room. Set against mirrored panels which reflect a dramatic city skyline, the screen appears to float within the space. Appliances and accessories are hidden away in the cupboard below. The choice of a black, semi-matt finish allows it to visually recede. A faux suede lends good looks and wearability to the big comfortable armchairs.

that are high-definition capable. But because of their bulk and weight, the larger sizes are best avoided.

## DIGITAL TELEVISION (DTV)

Digital television (DTV) is a broadcasting technology that offers superior picture quality (including wide-screen format) and sound to analogue transmission, as well as possibilities for broader content and interactive viewing. But the arrival of DTV doesn't mean kissing goodbye to your trusty old telly. While some newer models have built-in digital tuners to receive DTV, any standard set can access digital transmission by plugging it into a stand-alone digital tuner box. A wide-screen television, however, will maximise the visual impact of DTV.

### HOME THEATRE

- A dedicated room for a home theatre is the ideal. Acoustics-wise, a rectangular room is best, with viewing towards one of the shorter walls. By insulating walls, laying carpet and using heavy curtaining, you should also improve sound quality.
- There are budget options, like the space-conscious mini systems 'in a box', which can be placed on shelves in a living room, but these won't stack up against component systems, which offer considerably higher quality.
- Receivers with digital surround sound formats (Dolby Digital and Digital Theatre System) offer superior separation and clarity.
- Increasingly, the home PC linked to a broadband connection will be able to deliver games, movies and music, making it an integral part of the home theatre system.
- Consider a control system which can dim the lights, swish the curtains and roll the action, all while you're comfortably seated.

## SPEAKERS

Speakers are becoming increasingly svelte. Where a home is unfinished, speakers can be recessed into walls and ceilings, with wiring hidden within the cavities.

Speaker placement, however, is an art. The size and shape of a room, the surfaces within it and even the arrangement of furniture all come into play.

Positioning of some speakers is less critical because of their wide distribution of sound. These are the best choice if seating is much closer to one of the speakers, as you'll still be able to hear the second speaker for stereo balance.

In most cases, speakers recessed in the ceiling give the best sound coverage for background music, while speakers placed either side of the main focal point in a room, such as a fireplace or a picture window, are the best configuration for foreground sound. For open-plan areas, you may require more than one set of speakers for smooth sound coverage.

With surround sound for home theatre set-ups, speaker placement is less critical by virtue of having five speakers, plus the sub-woofer, and therefore more exposure to sound. The central speaker, which handles dialogue, should be placed either above or below the screen.

The left and right front speakers handle musical content and should be placed in the same way as stereo speakers. The rear speakers should be placed either side of the seating area, preferably slightly behind it and at ear level, while the sub-woofer (which handles very low bass) can be tucked away to either side, as bass sounds are non-directional.

Where speaker wire can't be run through wall and ceiling cavities or under the floor, use flat cable designed for under-carpet applications. Cable can be run up the walls in conduit, or with flat ribbon tape that adheres to the wall and can be painted or papered over. But you can save all of this work by choosing wireless speakers.

### 1. TV ON CALL

A wall-mounted television reads as just another element in an interior where black details – from the wrought iron of the bed to the leather upholstery of the swivel chair – play a defining role. A wireless connection allows the television in this bedroom to remotely access the video and DVD in the living room, providing the whole entertainment experience without doubling on appliances.

### 2. UNCLUTTERED

The miniaturisation of electronics has obvious benefits for their subtle integration into a room. Here, wall-mounted entertainment units manage to look svelte and uncluttered, with wiring routed through the wall cavity and speakers recessed into the ceiling. In this way, the floor is kept free of gear. By positioning the television on an adjustable bracket, it allows for comfortable viewing from the adjacent kitchen as well as the immediate sitting area. The contrast of black components against the white of the walls ties in with the clean-cut, Asian-style decorating theme.

### 3. VIEW THE REPEATS

When designing storage for audio-visual equipment, take your cues from other features within a room to create cohesion. Here, a plasma screen is integral to the symmetry of this elongated wall unit, with an appliance cupboard forming its mirror image around a central fireplace. DVDs and CDs are filed in a second cupboard at far right. Surround sound speakers are recessed in the bulkhead above the unit and in the ceiling behind the seating area.

Contemporary comfort is created by combining richly textured fabrics in an interesting, eclectic way. A grand bookcase, rather than a television screen, dominates this room. Windows are elegantly draped, rather than hung with lengths of fabric, in a Tuscan-country style.

The most wonderful part of putting together a room's scheme is when you reach the point of adding the really decorative elements. It's these decorations that deliver the visual excitement of colour and texture. The careful selection of big-ticket items for the floors and the walls — rugs, carpets and artworks, both large and small — is part of the process of giving your home its individual personality. Add to this the interplay of interesting accessories, and any room is well on its journey towards fulfilment.

1 | 2

### 1. CASUAL SISAL

Modern production methods have turned sisal and coir into stylish alternatives to carpet, but they can also make wonderful rugs when bound or edged with fabric. Coir is coarser and less expensive than sisal, but both can be used for heavy traffic areas. Sisal has a flatter weave than coir, making it softer underfoot. Strong sunlight will eventually cause the quite deep colours to fade. In this country weekender, sisal rugs enhance the understated elegance. An old trolley from a textile factory serves as a coffee table.

### 2. TUFTS ENOUGH

During the psychedelic '60s, pop culture embraced hot colours and geometric patterns, rya rugs from Denmark, flokatis from Greece and wall-to-wall shag carpet. Those influences are seen in many of the brilliant, hand-tufted wool rugs being created today for contemporary interiors. This long-pile, handcrafted rug from Spain is lush and inviting – it makes you want to run your fingers (as well as your toes) through its luscious locks.

# LAY DOWN A RUG

A RUG CAN BE SO MUCH MORE THAN A PRACTICAL SOLUTION TO PROVIDING SOFTNESS UNDERFOOT. A WEAVER DESIGNS A RUG TO BE A WORK OF ART AND SOMETHING TO CHERISH. CHOOSE ONE THAT SHOWS YOUR APPRECIATION OF THEIR CREATIVE EXPRESSION.

It's thought that hand-knotted rugs began with the nomadic tribes of Central Asia. These people were unwilling to kill valuable livestock to make floor coverings from their hides and pelts, so they used sheep, goat or camel hair to create textiles with a hair-like pile which imitated the texture and warmth of an animal hide.

Proof that rug-making was around as early as 400BC came 55 years ago, when the hand-knotted Pazryk 'carpet' was found in a royal tomb in Siberia – it's a striking testament to the weaver's art that it remained intact.

However the handmade rug came into being, it has since flourished. Rug weaving has developed into a highly sophisticated art form, but one that also produces a practical home furnishing.

## HANDMADE VS MACHINE-MADE

The biggest cost in producing a handmade rug is the enormous amount of labour involved. It's no surprise then that people have worked hard to make similar-looking rugs using power looms.

Today, however, new hand-tufting techniques, larger knot sizes and more streamlined production is seeing many handmade rugs competing with machine-made rugs on price.

The quality of materials and the dyeing techniques used directly affect the price of a rug. Wool and silk are the most expensive materials; cotton and synthetics like nylon and polypropylene are cheaper. Most new rugs are coloured using chemical dyes, but there is also a trend to using older-style, more expensive vegetable dyes to create subtle colours.

**3. RUGS AS ART**
In a contemporary sense, a rug is like a big splashy painting; something that resembles the artwork of children. And if it has no pedigree, then a rug should be used to bring comfort and colour to a room, rather than being admired for its investment value. Here, a hand-tufted woollen rug from Scandinavia introduces a brilliant boost of colour to a casual living room.

3

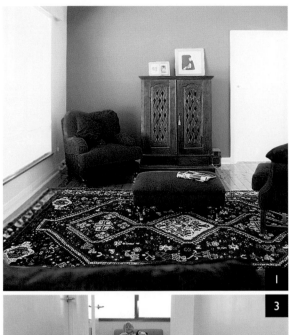

### 1. CLASSIC PERSIAN

Deep red and blue are the most popular background colours of a Persian rug. High quality hand-knotted rugs look better the more they age – in fact, a 10-year-old rug is deemed 'new' by dealers. There's a wide variety available in wool – both handmade and machine-made. Because the colours used are rich and the patterns symbolic, a Persian rug can dominate a space. In this small sitting room, the chenille velvet upholstery ties in the colour theme while toning down the pattern.

### 2. A MODERN KILIM

During the 18th century, entrepreneurs travelled to Turkey and Persia to commission rugs in the pastel colours and floral designs preferred by Europeans. It was at this point, when demand affected design, that rug weaving truly became an industry as we know it today. Here, a kilim is the centre of attention, drawing all other decorative elements together with its powerful, contemporary design and rich colour.

### 3. STEPPING SOFTLY

Hallways can be long, boring spaces, but you can make them a lot more interesting with a rug or runner. Here is a clever concept for introducing colour and style to a connecting hall in a modern family home. Plush pile rugs – designed in the style of Scandinavia's classic rya rugs – are placed in stepping stone fashion, giving tremendous visual clout and a toasty touch for littlies' bare feet.

### 4. BEDROOM WARMTH

Rugs are much like furniture in that they come in many degrees of quality and beauty. They range from handcrafted but mass-produced items to carefully crafted replicas of exquisite masterpieces, good 'old' rugs with 'worn' charm, and the man-made and mass-produced 'designer' rug. In this sleek bedroom, a rug is essential for warming toes where there is only bare floorboards.

**5. DOING A RUNNER**
For hallways and entries to feel more welcoming, a rug or runner offers softness underfoot. You can find many modern styles of runners, but the classic designs of a Persian rug are highly desirable and transcend fashion. They look especially good over pale waxed floorboards, as you can see in the hall of this older-style home.

and regions so the colours vary from country to country.

**RAG:** Rag rugs go back to 17th-century Scandinavia and Germany. They are made from pieces of fabric looped or stitched together using odds and ends. They can also be custom-made from fabric which matches other furnishings.

**RYA:** This is a brightly coloured high-pile rug from Denmark and Finland. Rya rugs were popular in the 1960s and are often oval-shaped.

**FLOKATI:** Originating in Greece, these rugs are made from heavy, shaggy, long-pile wool, traditionally in white or off-white. They were fashionable during the 1970s and are again popular.

**NEEDLEPOINT/TAPESTRY:** These flat-weave rugs are produced by sewing a detailed design or picture into a large piece of fabric. Various stitches can be used to create different patterns.

**HOOKED:** A hooked rug is a cross between a needlepoint and a pile rug. By varying the height of the loops in the weaving process, a sculptured effect is produced.

**TUFTED:** This pile yarn is wrapped around the warp threads, but is not tied. The pile is secured in place by coating the back of the rug with a latex type adhesive. The rug often looks very similar to a traditional knotted rug. The famous Tai Ping rugs are hand-tufted by skilled artisans in Hong Kong.

## RUG STYLES

Each culture has its own style of rug so there is a huge variation in weave, finish, colour and treatment. Generally speaking, there are flat-weave and traditional pile rugs. Pile rugs are usually thick and look more lush; flat-weave rugs are thinner.

**ORIENTAL:** The term 'oriental' simply means from the East, but it's commonly applied to hand-knotted, flat-weave rugs produced in the area stretching from the Balkans, over Turkey to North Africa, Iran, Central Asia and on to China.

**PERSIAN:** Persian rugs are usually made of wool, camel hair or silk. The most common Persian motifs are those with flowers, linked by tendrils and designs including animals and people. There are as many variations of the Persian rug as there are cities and villages in Iran.

**AUBUSSON:** This flat-weave style of woollen rug was first produced in France in the 17th century. Colours are delicate with detailed floral designs.

**DHURRIE:** The word 'dhurrie' is Indian for 'flat-weave'. A dhurrie is usually made from cotton and is easy to clean.

**KILIM:** This is the Persian word for 'flat-weave'. This style of rug, made in several countries including Turkey, Iran, Tibet and Morocco, is woven from thick wool. Kilim designs represent different tribes

## RUG CARE AND MAINTENANCE

### General care

- Good underlay extends a rug's life, but avoid placing a rug over thick pile carpet.
- Exposure to sunlight eventually fades rugs; a 180-degree rotation helps it fade evenly.
- Moths are a worry – move your rug frequently and keep it well aired.
- Keep pot plants away from rugs – seepage or condensation from the bottom of the plant causes the rug's foundation and pile to rot.

### Cleaning

- When a spill occurs, act immediately. Never rub, always blot – with paper towel, sponge or a clean cloth, adding cold (never hot) water in small quantities. Soda water or diluted mild detergent can also be used. Avoid soaking the rug, as this can cause mildew and the deterioration of threads. Blot until all moisture is gone.
- Vacuum regularly (once a week) in the direction of the nap of the rug. Never vacuum a fringe as the pulling can cause it to tear. Silk rugs should be vacuumed very gently once a fortnight, using a hand-held, flat-edged vacuum tool and smoothly sweeping in the direction of the pile.
- Orientals should be professionally washed every three to five years (silks every one or two years). Never steam or chemically clean these rugs, because both these methods strip the natural oils out of the wool pile, making the fibres more brittle and prone to wear.

### 1. SOUND ADVICE

Always use underlays on bare floors to stop a rug from moving around. Where rugs are specified for apartments, an underlay is crucial for added sound insulation. Penthouses like this one are designed to stand out from the crowd, but few enjoy 360-degree views. This sculptured, plush woollen rug was custom-designed to echo the curves and style of the swish apartment.

### 2. RAG TRADING

Rag rugs have their origins in Europe and were also popular in North America. For today's decorating, the rag rug is interpreted in suede and is machine-made and washable, with a sturdy backing. This rug resembles ticker-tape or shredded paper and creates a stylish zone around which elegant furniture is grouped.

### SELECTING A RUG

A rug can assume the central role in your decorating scheme. Use it in combination with other flooring materials, or as one big cover-up for the floor. A narrow rug (runner) will give comfort and direction to a set of stairs and make a hallway more welcoming. It's important to buy the most beautiful and best-crafted rug that you can afford. Quality counts: a cheap rug can look shabby in a matter of months, while a better-made item can keep its good looks and value for decades.

Rugs generally have never diminished in popularity – unlike carpet which falls in and out of favour with alarming regularity – because they offer so much more versatility in their colour, size and pattern. But their very best asset is that they can be quickly rolled up and taken with you when you move house.

### 1. SMOOTH CUT PILE

Cut pile is created by cutting the tops of the loops so they stand upright and make an even surface. You'll often see this type of carpet described as velour, plush or velvet, and it's most commonly laid in bedrooms. It was an excellent choice for this bedroom which opens directly into a spacious ensuite. The 'smooth' carpet and limestone-like floor tiles blend, both in finish and colour.

### 2. IN THE LOOP

It's important to match the quality of your carpet to its use, however in a bedroom you can choose a carpet graded as light duty, as there is far less foot traffic. The secret to softness underfoot is investing in a good underlay. In this bedroom, a multi-level loop-pile carpet – which has a sculptured look and doesn't show up footprints – forms a neutral backdrop to vintage textiles and an eclectic furniture collection.

# THE MAGIC OF CARPETS

WHAT'S DOING THE HARD YARDS FOR A FAMILY FLOOR? IT'S CARPET – NOW MAKING A WELCOME RETURN TO LIVING AREAS AS WELL AS BEDROOMS.

As we knock down walls and open up our houses to create brighter, light-filled spaces, noise and heat insulation have increasingly become an issue. Carpeting does loads to improve this situation, providing hush and helping to even out temperatures from day to night.

But probably what accounts more for carpet's popularity is its unashamed, toe-curling comfort. In a time when tactile sensitivity is big news on the home front, carpet is the only soft, warm flooring option that encourages you to slip off your shoes and pad barefoot, or lie down and stretch out.

Your carpet choice usually depends on your home's decor and the amount of foot traffic the carpet will receive. In contemporary homes, pattern tends to obscure the strong form of architecture and furniture so a neutral, textured carpet or plain-coloured, smooth hard-twist style are appropriate. Country-style schemes are complemented by a strongly textured carpet like wool sisal, and rooms with a romantic mood call for wonderfully plush pile carpets or those with a European-style pattern.

Generally, cut pile is considered more formal than loop pile and loop pile inevitably wears longer than cut pile, although any good quality carpet should last well past a decade.

Carpet grading determines wearability – medium duty suits areas not prone to constant traffic, heavy duty works in hallways and big family living rooms, and extra heavy duty is for all intense traffic areas.

Whatever fibre your carpet is made from, whether it be wool, a wool blend, a synthetic polypropylene or a natural fibre like coir, sisal and jute – it must be hard-working for today's flexible and highly spirited lifestyle.

5

## 1. FAMILY VALUE

Carpet has to be practical for family living. You have to know it can be cleaned easily and look good – always. This waterfront home, revamped for more family-friendly living, reveals a wonderfully textured, pale sisal carpet. It gives a nice feel underfoot while providing visual texture and a low maintenance surface.

## 2. CLEANING UP

Make sure when you decide on your carpet you buy a good vacuum cleaner. A straight suction vacuum cleaner is ideal for loop pile, and an upright with a revolving brush-head suits a cut pile. Grit plus friction cuts woollen fibres, so ensure outdoor areas are swept and the grit doesn't get inside into the carpet. In this home, a deep indigo, cut-pile, hard-twist woollen carpet gives depth and richness to an all-white theme.

## 3. IN THE BLEND

Integrated indoor/outdoor living requires a clever hand in blending furnishings. The sleek grey palette in this kitchen is enhanced by flooring which sees polished marble tiles meeting low-pile sable-coloured carpet. The balcony in the foreground is laid with honed bluestone.

## 4. USE SAMPLES

When you're looking around for carpets, make sure you take home the largest available carpet samples to see how they look down on your floor. And as you do with paint samples, view them in different lighting situations, as colours and textures alter from day to night. In this living room, the designer has opted for a haute couture mix of 'twilight' colours and tailored patterns. A flat-weave synthetic Maslan carpet gives the touch and look of fabric to the floor.

## 5. COLOUR DRAMA

Today's contemporary schemes suit many styles of carpet. A smooth, wool hard-twist in a bold, plain colour, like this rust-red carpet, can be used with confidence to achieve drama – particularly when it's matched with some great artwork or deeply coloured walls. Fading can occur in any carpet – it's the dye's reaction to sunlight – and here the owner has installed a sunscreen blind to filter the light.

## CLEVER CARPETING

- Awkward elements in a room can be camouflaged by choosing a carpet in the same shade as the walls.
- Pale carpets will lighten a dark room while earth-hued carpets take the chill off a room lacking sunshine.
- The chic newer neutrals will offset a bright painting or tone down furnishings.
- Blues are ideal for rooms with plenty of sun.
- If accidental spills and rough and tough wear drive you nuts, go for a patterned carpet.
- Avoid large areas of pattern if you don't want a room to close in.
- Remember about pattern overload – this can occur when 'architectural' patterns like brickwork, leadlight windows or ornate mouldings intrude on your scheme.
- There is an abundance of 'natural' imitations on the market – some wool imitations can trick the eye, but rarely will they also deceive the touch.
- If buying an apartment off the plan, make sure the carpet quality is specified, otherwise take the money value and buy your own carpet. Display apartment carpet may sometimes be substituted with a carpet of lesser quality but similar appearance, which will have to be replaced prematurely.

### 1. SENSUAL TYPES

A frise or hard-twist pile carpet gives a touch of luxury with its textured cut-pile effect and is an excellent choice for a living room. Here, a mocha-coloured, hard-twist, plush-pile carpet elegantly enforces the subtle monotonal colour scheme, and complements the modular seating's sensuous suede upholstery.

### 2. HUE'S THERE

Carpeting is a great option for apartment living because of its acoustic properties. A small space can be made to look more streamlined when you take the carpet beyond the bedroom and into the living area, as seen here. While deep, dark colours are fine, beware of stripes, checks and bold patterns, as they tend to overpower a small room. Here, a luscious red plush-pile carpet gives great depth and character.

### 3. PATTERN HOOK

Some people find patterned carpets bring back bad vibes – memories of yesteryear are not always inspirational. But patterned carpets today are a different breed altogether from those over-the-top designs commonplace 30 years ago. These days, a patterned carpet brings a richness and sense of intimacy to larger spaces. They don't have to be theatrical, ditsy or downright boring. This sophisticated leaf-and-trellis design doesn't compete with the other furnishings and complements the colour theme.

# ART IN THE HOME

A PAINTING OR SCULPTURE IN THE HOME IS OFTEN CONSIDERED A 'DECORATION' AS MUCH AS A PIECE OF ART. YOU BUY A WORK AND HANG IT IN A PARTICULAR PLACE IN THE HOME TO EVOKE AN EMOTION, BUT QUITE OFTEN IT ALSO SERVES TO COMPLEMENT A COLOUR SCHEME OR HIGHLIGHT AN ARCHITECTURAL FEATURE.

### 1. A BROAD SWEEP

If you want a light, airy feel for your home, choose large pieces for your walls. In this case, an abstract in muted earth tones complements the rich chocolate and spice colours of the decor and bedroom furnishings. Although it is large, this painting does not overwhelm; it 'whispers' rather than 'screams', giving the other design elements of the bedroom their due.

Art is an expression both by the artist and by the person who buys their work. When you consider how dramatically art can change the whole ambience of a room, it makes sense then to allow for it in your decorating budget.

Spend on artworks as you would on top-quality new carpets or curtains, and enjoy the fact that a piece of art is far more versatile in the home. Art can 'travel' easily from room to room, style to style, and from house to house. It's an heirloom for generations, and it's always a talking point.

If you find yourself growing tired of a work, move it to another space and start the metamorphosis all over again. Of course, the fact that good art can be a wise financial investment is also appealing.

## CREATING IMPACT

Choosing an artwork to suit you and your home can sometimes be a complex process, but not always; many people simply stumble across things that they love. It should always be remembered that art is ultimately in the eye of the beholder – if something strikes a chord with you, it's usually bound to look 'right' in your home.

But balance your tastes with the state of the market, and be choosy – it is far better to own a few quality pieces than to possess several second-rate ones.

### 2. FOCUS PULLER

Bold, contemporary pieces work well in minimalist spaces. If you have chosen simple lines and an uncluttered feel in your decor, make your walls do the talking with clean and arresting visuals. Contemporary artworks are rarely subtle, and will always provide a talking point – but as they create such a strong focus, choose wisely. Continue the theme with a series of images for extra impact.

### 1. GROUP WORK

Rather than having just one major piece, a group of several can create a lot of interest. But be aware that composition is all-important. These mixed sketches have been hung quite low, and arranged both vertically and horizontally. Different shapes and frames are mixed and matched to add depth. The result is an unusual yet compelling display which reflects the eclectic nature of the room.

### 2. REPETITION

A long white wall cries out for a gallery of artworks. This bold series of oils is titled 'The Six Seasons of Mars'. In interior design, repetition is a powerful tool, but it needs to be balanced with minimalist lines in order to be successful. Also remember, this approach does require uncluttered space.

### 3. SUM OF THE PARTS

Individual works can be grouped to form one large feature – there can never be an excess of art. This collection of 24 paintings by the one artist may be mixed and matched at whim. You could achieve an equally interesting effect by segmenting a large print to hang on the wall.

3

## CREATING MOOD

Always consider what 'mood' a piece will create in a space. This can be affected by the lighting, the wall and floor surfaces, existing furniture and fabric styles and the aspect of the room. Your choice of artwork should try to match the style of the room – if the decor is opulent, with plenty of antiques, something more classical will work best. If, on the other hand, you live in a warehouse conversion with minimalist furniture and an expanse of bare wall, a contemporary work may be preferable. Having said that, eclecticism is all about mixing styles and can work well, as long as there is an inherent link in colour or style between the art and where it will be situated.

## IS BIG BETTER?

These days, there is a trend toward large, modern pieces, driven primarily by the way interior design has focused on white walls and muted furnishings. Many artists are now consciously producing larger works to respond to the trend, and a massive painting on a feature wall will be undeniably impressive.

But a word of warning – don't buy something too big, as it will not only overwhelm a space, but be difficult to move about and hang.

## WHERE TO BUY ART

So where can you find that perfect artwork? If you are a novice, there's no better place to start the search than at an art fair. Gallery owners come together at these to display a selection of works by a range of artists. The beauty is you can view hundreds of artworks without being under the watchful eye of a gallery assistant in a space that's little bigger than a living room, so it's more casual.

## LOCATION, LOCATION

Grand-scale artworks have become popular, but it's important to get the look right. Don't allow the piece to be crowded – leave plenty of space around a work for it to 'breathe', especially if it's bright. Black-and-white works tend to draw in the eye so don't need as much space between them.

Hang the painting so its bottom is slightly higher than table height. When there's no furniture in a room to use as a guide, find the horizontal mid-line of the painting and hang it so it matches your line of sight when standing.

Hanging large works on white or off-white walls works well – but go carefully with coloured walls, as the effect can be overpowering.

## HANG IT ALL

Hanging art well is all about colour and balance; where you place a piece of art can make or break a room. You do need to do a bit of preparation beforehand. Don't use nails but, rather, picture hooks placed securely in the wall. Before hanging, examine the back of the painting to ensure that the hanging hardware is strong and secure. If the painting is framed, the hardware should be attached to the back of the frame, not to the stretcher or strainer. Things can become more complicated with contemporary paintings which don't have protective frames, and you may need to call in an expert.

A good picture-hanger is not a decorating indulgence – in Europe they are considered professionals, just like interior designers, and they can make even so-so artworks look fantastic. The benefits of hiring a professional aren't just aesthetic – both the equipment and know-how required to hang art, especially large pieces, is specialised.

A picture-hanger will take into account the weight of a piece, whether it will need support brackets, where the electrical wires are in the walls, and what condition the walls are in. A painting that isn't properly secured on a wall can be dangerous, so it's worth paying the money to have it done professionally.

### 1. GILT FEELINGS

Considered passé by some, classical art will nonetheless always have its place, but it does need to be in the right environment in order to shine. This room, with all the elements of a master bedroom in a country manor, has the sort of classic scale which can support 'grand' pictures. Their gilded frames and traditional subject matter blend majestically with the formal European-style bed, plush pile carpet and tapestry cushions.

### 2. PLACING SCULPTURE

A painting is not the only form of displayable art. You can create a very strong effect with sculpture. These African busts are highlighted by their position in wall recesses. It's a good idea to stick to a theme when you're displaying three-dimensional pieces; here, tribal motifs dominate the scheme.

### 3. A NAIVE EFFECT

Children take centre stage in this house: in the entrance area, toy cars double as sculpture and a giant, kid-friendly artwork dominates. What's interesting here is the use of colour. Vivid unframed canvases in kindergarten colours sit well in open spaces. As a rule of thumb, the cleaner the backdrop, the more impact the art will have.

### 4. CROSS CULTURAL

Blending the old with the new and mixing different styles can create a dramatic interior. The artworks on the walls here complement giant Central Asian and Middle Eastern sculptures. In this room, overscaled design is the key; anything petite would be lost.

There are enormous price variances, but it's possible to purchase a drawing or lithograph for hundreds rather than thousands of dollars.

If you are after a work by a particular artist, auctions are a great way to buy, and here again the price does not have to be prohibitive. Many Indigenous and contemporary artists sell in the five- to 10-thousand dollar mark, but you can get originals for less than that if you do your research and have a bit of luck on your side! Get in touch with the auction houses near you and ask to be included on their mailing list.

The other option when buying art is to go directly to the galleries. Here you'll be paying a gallery's commission and, consequently, the prices will be higher. Gallery owners and their staff understand the trepidations of the first-time buyer, so don't be afraid to ask plenty of questions.

Another tip: request a look in the stockroom, as it's a treasure trove of artworks that happen not to be showing at the time. Many collectors have found their dream piece deep in the bowels of a gallery. The only essential is that you are buying something you really love.

And don't forget about photography. Contemporary photography is still an emerging market in this country and some beautiful and moving images can be picked up for very reasonable prices. Visit a couple of specialist photographic galleries to see what is around.

Ultimately, art and how and where you place it in the home is limited only by your imagination. If your budget doesn't run to buying a major piece, it doesn't mean you must forgo one of life's pleasures. You can create a spectacular display from something you may never have considered, such as a series of bright children's paintings or a group of favourite objects that share a theme or colour.

Play with your art; move it from room to room, so that it's always alive and interesting. Whichever way you choose to decorate with art, the advice is the same – don't be afraid to experiment.

# SUCCESS WITH ACCESSORIES

IT IS THE SMALL THINGS – THE PHOTOS, THE GIFTS, BELOVED COLLECTIONS
OR A SINGLE FAVOURITE ORNAMENT – WHICH GIVE A HOME ITS SOUL.

Anyone who has ever sat in a room thinking that it resembled a museum – decorated to within an inch of its life – might question why such perfection was so devoid of personality. Well, it's probably because the personal, real-life expression is missing; those small but significant finishing touches and details which are added to a room to say 'your' style. Family keepsakes, framed photos, mementos, interesting collectables, books and flowers – these things should be a part of every home as they are of every life.

However, if each room in your house is crammed with photos, trinkets and souvenirs, you stand the chance of being labelled a hoarder and may need to pare back your possessions. On the other hand, a bare, minimalist environment may reveal you have a don't-care attitude for taking responsibility for anything worth collecting. Is it indicating you're concerned only with the here and now?

But do real families actually live comfortably in such pristine spaces? Everyone needs to be surrounded by things that make them feel good – it could be that collection of Matchbox cars hung onto since childhood or an array of exquisite, contemporary art glass, a stash of handmade boxes from your overseas adventures or a prized collection of crystal, sculpture or porcelain.

Your accessories may have no investment value other than they finish off the look of a room, personalise the space and make you feel fabulous about it. A couch full of colourful silk cushions or a table stacked with glossy art and design books may be the only accessories you want.

Remember, too, the current urge to liberate rooms by stripping them of the personal touch only works when there are things of great structural beauty within the room to admire. Without this, many rooms are boring boxes.

The secret behind the placement and display of accessories is to bear in mind proportion and balance. Unusual places such as window ledges or piano tops can accommodate eye-catching vignettes. Clustering objects together saves room and can make the grouping art in itself.

Make small groups to balance your rooms – but go easy on how many you have. If you suspect you have too much stuff and don't want to chuck it, change your arrangements seasonally; keep them on the move.

## 1. SAIL TABLE
Commonsense prevails when displaying impressive single items – essentially you find a spot where they can stand alone. This beautiful model yacht is seen in a good light all round on this table. It's also worth considering keeping the background free of any pattern or artwork so there's no distraction from a classic shape.

## 2. PATTERNS FOR LIFE
Plain white rooms tend to be tiring on the eye and a bit cold, so alter the temperature with accessories that bring in texture and pattern as well as accent colour. With its soul in the tropics, this entertaining room is loaded up with exciting accessories – leopard-print throws, cane baskets and a plethora of gilt-framed family photos. The mood is indeed exotic.

### 1. DISPLAY RULES

It's always good to place repetitive objects (plates of the same size, for instance) in an ordered row. Mix different heights for collections of only two or three items, otherwise there's a danger it will look more like a collection of wares at a garage sale than a display. There's a beautiful arrangement of accessories in this entrance hall, where lasting impressions count.

### 2. STEAL A REFLECTION

A mirror's capacity to bounce the light and hold a scene within its reflection makes it a dynamic decorating device. Place it to bring sunshine into a room or to enhance a corner with its captured 'scenes'. Here, a contemporary mirror livens up a cool white space with its reflections of the garden.

### 3. BOLD IS BETTER

Some accessories can be inherently exotic and vibrant – artefacts from Indigenous and other ancient cultures, for instance. Your eye will be drawn to the colour, texture and form – as in this display – if they're staged in front of a boldly painted wall: ochre, chocolate and rusty red are good. But where you group these items is vital; avoid putting them anywhere you might trip over them.

## MIRROR'S IMAGE

Mirrors have been used for centuries in the household and as objects of desire and decoration. Those big enough to reflect the entire body didn't appear until the 1st century AD. By the end of the Middle Ages, hand mirrors had become quite common throughout Europe, usually being made of silver, though sometimes of polished bronze. The method of backing a sheet of glass with a thin film of reflective tin and mercury became widespread in Venice during the 16th century – mirrors crafted in Venice were famous for their high quality and were extremely expensive.

Carved mirror frames were produced from around the 17th century and the tradition of incorporating a mirror into the space over the mantelpiece became established. Painted decoration replaced carving around mirrors by the end of the 1700s, when the French began making circular mirrors with neo-classic gilt frames – often supporting candlesticks. In the 19th century, the cheval glass mirror was created.

Today's mirrors are made by fusing molten aluminium or silver to the back of a plate of glass in a vacuum. Modern mirrors are seen in many guises, in both contemporary and traditional designs. When cleaning, avoid anything abrasive (this includes a sea-sponge). Clean with a chamois.

**1. WORDS' WORTH**
Think twice about getting rid of all your books when you're streamlining your rooms. They are essential to a family's sense of belonging and are a visual 'comfort factor' for children; they make great accessories and are a good source of colour in a room. Custom-made shelves like these mean flexible storage. It's important to remember to keep books out of direct sunlight as this will cause their spines to fade and warp.

HOME

### 2. BY THE BOOK

There's no use having all those books if you can't easily find them. Store your books alphabetically by author, title or topic – it's simpler than you think. Using a step stool or library ladder is imperative if you have a wall of books like this inspired collector and reader. Remember, books gather dust, and lots of books gather lots of dust. Learn to become skilful with a feather duster.

### 3. FIND A FOCUS

If you have a quirky mix of things, group them with an eye toward one feature – in this case, it's the mirror with its tailored woven leather frame. Sometimes the most stylish displays are objects shown in a new way. Here, a bagful of apples contained in an open wire basket finds balance between a delicate display of orchids and a bonsai.

### 4. MORE THAN POTS

Decorative ceramics have been an enduring source of pleasure for centuries, with roots that go back to the painted pottery of ancient times. You can choose from literally dozens of different styles to display in your home, each reflecting the charisma of the artisan. Here is a collection of colourful pots, jugs and plates – somewhat reminiscent of the whimsical majolica that was so loved during the Victorian era.

### 5. GRAB ATTENTION

Every home needs a bit of fun, something quizzical and vibrant, especially in the hall or entry. After all, for some people the whole point of having a dedicated entry is to make an impression. Think about using accessories to capture the eye – a pair of amusement-park clowns in front of painted panels makes an arresting display in a hallway.

### 1. CHINA CLASSIC

Pottery from China's Ming period was coloured with cobalt to create the distinctive blue-and-white designs so popular with collectors. Throughout this dynasty, the dragon and phoenix were the most used decorative motifs. The famous blue-and-white Willow pattern, often grouped with Ming pottery in a display, was developed by Josiah Spode in the late 18th century from an original Chinese pattern called Mandarin. Here, this owner, who is passionate about blue-and-white china, has opted for a 'more is better' approach.

### 2. WORKING CLASS

Give a small space personality with accessories that do double-duty. It's all the better if you can actually use the things which make your home individual. Never underestimate the decorative potential of the most utilitarian item — here, a classic hatstand becomes a stage for 'applying' colour and texture.

### 3. MAKE IT PERSONAL

Accessorising need not be governed by strict rules. Rooms gain more personality when items from different eras and styles are brought together. This quiet bedroom corner becomes a personal sanctuary with the addition of just a few well-loved pieces. A subtle blue theme unites an odd assortment of treasures including a lead-light lamp, candelabrum, antique oil painting and 1950s fan.

## FLOWER MATCH-MAKING

**Some simple ideas for arranging blooms.**

- Sculptural, large-scale arrangements can serve as an artwork, providing a room with colour and texture. For example, combine a single cascading *Heliconia* and tall Gymea-lily leaves in a narrow, straight-sided clear vase for drama in a big room.
- Give classic white blooms (like hydrangeas, roses and lilies) a twist by displaying them in modern, sculptural vases — organic shapes are very cool.
- Introduce a surprise element by 'containing' flowers in other decorative objects. For instance, fresh lavender in a basket or white roses in a traditional French wire birdcage.
- Experiment with unusual vessels — medicinal bottles, milk jugs, water carafes and salad bowls — to show off single blooms.

**Remember:**

- Change water every two days — add a drop of bleach to stop water from discolouring.
- Display your vases away from the fruit bowl. Ethylene gas from ripening fruit is not good for flowers — but to get flowers to open by a particular time, put them in a room with a bunch of ripe bananas!

3

The owner of this bedroom is passionate about vintage linens and, for her, comfort is all about a sumptuous bed, neutral colours, soft fabrics and beautiful flowers. The quilt on the bed and the tea-cloth on the side table were local market finds; the ruched austrian blind, pretty as a picture, is fitted merely for decoration.

A comfortable room should be both pleasing on the eye and practical. For most people, it takes a little planning and a lot of shopping to get the mix right. Your furniture should be as inviting as possible – sofas you want to dive into and tables that are big enough for you and your friends to settle around. Your bed is a personal nest, a respite from daily stress which offers the perfect place to regenerate your body and soul. Surround yourself with all the things you love, no matter whether they match or not. Remember that comfort is all about touch – the more we feel the more we relax, and the more we enjoy!

# BEST SEATS IN THE HOUSE

HAVING SOMEWHERE INVITING TO SIT IS THE SECRET OF A COMFORTABLE HOME.
SEATING IS THE CORE OF A LIVING AREA AND DEFINES THE STYLE OF A ROOM.
IT PAYS TO PUT YOUR MONEY INTO BUYING THE BEST YOU CAN AFFORD.

Much of a room's air of welcome and sense of comfort and style comes from the choice of seating and the way that it's arranged within a space.

Modern homes are geared to casual-style living and there has been a move away from the stuffiness of the three-piece suite and rooms full of formal, upright furniture. More flexible arrangements of sofas, ottomans and armchairs are better at meeting the varied demands of today's multi-functional, open-plan spaces.

The sofa consumes a sizeable chunk of the living area, strongly influencing any decorating agenda and forming the core of the seating placement. You can create a contemporary mood and make a room seem more spacious with a sleek, low-line sofa or one that's raised off the floor on legs. Tight upholstery will give a neat, tailored effect for a more formal look.

Take cues from the proportions of the room. Small-scale pieces feel lost in a cavernous space, while high-backed seating would clutter a room where the ceilings are low. Curved or rounded seating can play down the angular lines of a boxy room, while awkwardly shaped areas can benefit from the flexibility of modular designs.

To be truly comfortable, however, the style of sofa should reflect its intended use: a high back where head support is needed, high arms for propping up against or low, wide arms for resting your head on. Low seating can be difficult for some people to negotiate, while a taller body will benefit from a deep seat.

### 1. MODULAR OPTIONS

Modular seating tends to offer the best fit where there's limited space or an awkward floor plan. This leather-covered sectional sofa is sized to the length of the wall and shaped into an L to cordon off the sitting area within an open living space. At the same time, the low-rise section maintains an open feel to the seating arrangement. A predominantly white palette, warmed by measured doses of red, gives the interior a calm quality.

### 2. A BIT FUNKY

Modern decorating embraces the mismatched, the one-off and the mix of old and new. While large-scale furniture is often chosen to blend into a scheme, an occasional chair can be more extroverted. This funky floral fabric would be too loud for a large sofa, but gives this 1950s chair its charismatic poise. Although retro elements define this interior, the look is decidedly fresh and modern.

### 1. FRENCH STYLE

Bare legs, scrolled arms and rounded backs are the requisites of French salon-style seating. While chunky, squared-off designs can easily overwhelm a small space, furniture with a fine line and gentle curves adds a light touch and softens the angles of box-like rooms. Red fabric gives this sofa a theatrical touch, and leather-upholstered club chairs add the required tone of luxury. For a style that demands attention to detail, the shape and finish of chair and sofa legs should coordinate or harmonise.

When working out your seating requirements, bear in mind that two people will generally shy away from sharing a two-seater sofa unless they are on familiar terms, so a three-seater design is much more practical. A sofa combined with two or three smaller upholstered pieces creates a comfortable conversational grouping in a room.

A well-made piece is the key to lasting good looks, comfort and support. Search for upholstered seating that has a solid hardwood frame, traditional coil springs and quality stuffing, and choose upholstery fabrics that can take the knocks and spills of everyday life. Choosing a fabric in a neutral colour will prevent a sofa from overwhelming a space and will allow it to ride out any subsequent changes in decorating style.

While pragmatism plays a strong role in the choice of a sofa, occasional chairs offer you greater scope for decorative expression. Here's an opportunity to showcase a luxurious fabric, have a play with pattern or colour, or introduce a whimsical form – the individual touches that bring a room to life.

### 2. MODERN LINES

A contemporary-style sofa typically has square arms, a low, straight back and slender legs to complement the clean lines and open feel of the modern interior. Here, cobalt blue upholstery adds a touch of richness to an otherwise pared-back space. An ottoman offers a more flexible, less bulky alternative to a second sofa. Silk cushions add a touch of oriental colour.

### 3. IN THE GROOVE

Sculptural seating works well in a spacious interior. The swivel bases of these mid-20th-century chairs allow for a quick change of focus from the wall-mounted plasma screen to the sweeping vistas offered by this penthouse apartment. A circular rug anchors what might otherwise seem like a loose arrangement of seating. Designs are extrovert enough to catch the eye, but do not distract from the all-important view.

### 4. MAKE A NEAT FIT

Carefully configured to fit an alcove-like space between a staircase and wall, this modular, slab-style seating creates a strongly architectural look, with colour used to signal the different layers. The design is low-slung in response to the recess cut into the end wall, while steel legs lend an overall lightness to the effect.

### 5. COLOUR SHOTS

Brightly coloured upholstery plays up the quirky shape of these cushioned bar stools. In an interior where white predominates, their small jolts of colour work as visual punctuation marks without upsetting the overall sense of calm. The suede-look fabric is sensual, hard-wearing and able to be spot cleaned. For a space more exposed to the workings of the kitchen, however, wipeable timber or metal would be better.

## TAKING A SEAT

**Initially bulky, upholstered seating evolved by the mid-18th century into the designs we see today.**

**CHAISE-LONGUE** is an elegant upholstered chair associated with the Regency period, having an elongated back and seat for reclining and an arm at one end only.

**CHESTERFIELD** is a classic English seating style, often leather-upholstered, with deep button tufting and large rolled arms at the same height as the back. It adds a formal, masculine tone to a traditional interior.

**CLUB** is a classic from the Art Deco period (1910 to 1939). The curved-back, upholstered chair has sloping arms and wooden legs. Typically finished in velvet or leather, it is the archetypal bar, library or study chair.

**LADDERBACK** is a country-style wooden chair designed with several horizontal slats or rails across its back. It's often in the form of a high-back chair with a rush seat. The spindle-backed Windsor is another classic country piece.

**LOUIS XV** is a French neo-classical style from the 18th century. Gently curved and partially upholstered (often in silk or velvet), this chair has open arms and legs carved with motifs such as flowers, shells and scrolls. It's a perennially popular accent chair.

**WINGBACK** is a fully upholstered chair dating from the 17th century with a high back, stuffed arms and cabriole legs. The wings protrude at head height and offer protection from draughts and fireside heat. An ideal reading chair.

### 1. CHOOSE A STOOL
With the trend towards more casual modes of dining and entertaining, the bar stool has come of age. Sleek styling, however, needn't be uncomfortable. A backrest, contoured seat and foot rail make sitting on a stool much more comfortable. Stool height should be compatible with the benchtop, providing a minimum knee clearance of 30cm and allowing elbows to rest comfortably on the counter.

### 2. HIGH-FIBRE SEATING
Where neutral tones reign, texture becomes a key decorative element. Wicker, rattan, water hyacinth, seagrass and other plant fibres produce seating that is wonderfully tactile. These dining chairs, with seats woven in abaca leaf, catch the eye with their textural detail and slight variation of tone, but without overwhelming the space. A glass-topped table provides an exciting contrast.

### 3. MODERN COUNTRY
Modern country style is a clean, uncluttered look that embraces natural materials and handcrafted touches. The rush-seated ladderback is a classic country chair often found in kitchens and dining rooms, but its lightness allows it to be seconded to other rooms in the house.

### 4. A MORE CASUAL MIX
In line with more casual styles of eating, dining-room furniture has lost much of its starchy airs and graces. A table surrounded by a mix of seating rather than a regiment of cloned chairs makes for a more relaxed look. Here, an oak bench contrasts with three leather chairs on opposite sides of an oak table. Timber and leather has a robust, wipe-down practicality for an informal family dining area.

### 5. SLIP-COVERS ARE IN
Breezy white slip-covers are a practical option for living with white. Slip-covers are also ideal for disguising worn upholstery, protecting finishes from dust and sunlight, and unifying mismatched furniture.

2 3
4 5

### 1. NEW KITCHEN CHAIRS

More than a utility space, the modern kitchen is geared for eating and entertaining, and stools and chairs are integral to the design. The height of the workbench will dictate the required seat height; as a rule of thumb, about 60cm for a 90cm-high standard bench or 75cm for a 108cm raised workbench. For an integrated look, choose stools and chairs in height variations of the same design. Finishes should complement those used for the worktop, cupboard doors, handles or appliances, for example.

### 2. THE ARRANGEMENT

Voluminous spaces require similarly scaled furniture to achieve a sense of harmony and balance. Invariably, the largest piece will face the room's focal point, here the fireplace and television, while the arrangement as a whole should channel traffic so it minimises intrusion into the sitting area. The graphic print used for the beanbags adds textural interest, with a measured jolt of lime from the armchairs. The blond bentwood side tables can function equally well as stools.

### 3. CONFIDENCE PLUS

Black-and-tan striped sofas, animal-print cushions and a leather chesterfield make for a sophisticated masculine look in this apartment living room. The boldness of the stripe lends a confident air, while the attention to detail, from the piping to the leather trim, ensures the sofas stand up to scrutiny from all angles. Here the back of one sofa is clearly on view, in an arrangement that creates a division between living and dining zones. Tight upholstery adds to the tailored look, with minimal need for plumping and smoothing.

### 4. KEEP IT SLEEK

Seating takes on a sculptural role in the white, gallery-like spaces of the minimalist interior. Sleek, low-slung and firmly upholstered designs sit most comfortably within these streamlined roomscapes, where furniture tends to be restricted to a few large-scale pieces. A modern version of the daybed or chaise-longue, this sectional sofa also has a backless partner that can function as an ottoman when located more centrally within a room.

3

4

## CLEANING LEATHER

- Pigmented leather has been treated with a protective finish to resist soiling and staining, making it the best choice for a family with young children. Aniline leather (distinguished by its natural markings and colour variations), Nubuck (a brushed aniline) and suede demand extra care as they have minimal or no protective coating. Being softer, they are more prone to scuffing and general wear and tear, too.

- A weekly clean should prevent a build-up of dust, grime and body oils to keep your upholstery looking good. A robust leather can be vacuumed gently with a soft brush attachment, but use a duster or dry cloth on aniline and Nubuck. Next, wipe the upholstery in gentle circular movements with a clean, barely damp cloth, paying attention to areas that have direct contact with the body. A weak solution of mild, non-detergent soap or an approved cleaning spray can be used for this.

- For suede and Nubuck, specialist brushes and cloths help remove light soiling or dried stains and will revive a flattened nap.

- Three to four times a year, apply a leather conditioner and protector after normal cleaning. In most cases, stain removal is best tackled by a specialist. Vigorous rubbing can remove the dye and permanently damage the leather.

- Only use approved leather-care products. General-purpose cleaners can cause the leather to crack, discolour or become sticky. Always follow the cleaning recommendations outlined in the warranty.

1

### 1. ONE FOR THE KIDS

There's plenty of room for fun furniture in a playroom. This blazing red sofa has a cartoonish quality that complements the room's theme and provides a comfy place to curl up with a book or a bunny. Hard pointed edges were avoided and the sofa legs were removed to make the seating a child-friendly height. Tight yet well-cushioned upholstery is in a fabric that can take the knocks.

### 2. COUNTRY FABRICS

Traditional country-style interiors are classic and comforting. Florals, simple checks and stripes, plaids, small all-over patterns and plains are preferred to shiny or highly textured fabrics. Often a pretty multi-coloured floral will inspire the colour scheme, with the lightest hue repeated on the walls. Here, the red check of the wingback chair links with the red in the sofa's floral fabric.

### 3. A TOUCH OF FLORAL

Occasional chairs, also called accent or exposed-wood chairs, offer scope for experimenting with more luxurious upholstery treatments, as they demand less fabric. They serve as focal points without dominating a scheme. French-style furniture is favoured for its lightness and elegance and this Louis XV chair captures the colours of Provence among furnishings that add layers of texture, colour and mellowness to a cool, modern interior.

### 4. ETHNIC FLAIR

A dining setting that features a mix of materials is far more interesting than a perfectly matched set. Here, identical chairs sport different prints of African Mali mudcloth to assert their individuality without straying far from the fold. Ethnic designs and details like this imbue a modern space with a touch of the handcrafted. The table's tortoiseshell finish adds further richness.

# TABLE TALKING

AS THE WAY WE LIVE BECOMES MORE INFORMAL, THE ROLE OF THE TABLE HAS CHANGED. IT HAS BEEN ABSORBED INTO THE GENERAL LIVING SPACE AND IS NO LONGER RESERVED ONLY FOR EATING.

The rise of the open-plan layout has seen the demise of the dining room. Its formal airs and graces are largely out of sync with more casual modes of living, and in the competition for precious space, it has lost ground to the demands of a home office or home theatre.

Not that the dining table itself is under threat. Gathering around a table to enjoy a hearty meal with family and friends remains one of life's most pleasurable rituals. But being absorbed into the general living space of the open-plan home means the dining table must serve as a multi-functional surface, where homework, household accounts and other activities can be accommodated.

## HARD-WORKING

The dining table is usually out on show, so it needs to combine good looks with practicality. Favourite materials include timber, glass, stone and laminate. Polished concrete, though heavy, looks beautiful. Glass-topped designs, however, can quickly become fingermarked, and cutlery clatters on their surface, so they aren't the best choice for households with young children.

## SPACE CONSCIOUS

Responding to the lightness of modern living spaces, tables have become ever more slim and seemingly lightweight. Straight, slender legs or simple pedestal or frame bases create designs that seem to float. A reflective tabletop (glass, mirrored, metallic, polished marble) will bounce light and visually recede, making a tight space seem less cluttered, while tables that are entirely transparent slip easily into any style of room.

## 1. HEIRLOOMS APPARENT

Juxtaposing antique or heirloom pieces with contemporary furniture creates great interest. Set alongside crisply upholstered Louis XV chairs, an old ship's cargo-hold door gives dimension to a glass-topped coffee table and adds textural richness to the room's palette of neutrals. Beautifully carved or patinated temple doors from Bali, China or Japan also make decorative and original tabletops.

## 2. THEATRE DINER

Theatrical touches take the dining experience out of the everyday. A setting of antique Jacobean-style chairs and a marble-topped table with a wrought-iron base creates a baronial feel, enhanced by the oriental carpet and coats of arms on the wall. Placing the table beside glazed french doors ensures plenty of sunlight for daytime dining.

### 3. FORMAL WEAR

Red is said to stimulate the appetite and encourage conversation, making it the colour of choice for a formal dining room. Free of the practical constraints imposed on everyday meals areas, these rooms can indulge in highly polished surfaces, precious fabrics and touches that are just for show. Here, high-backed, upholstered seating teams with a dark timber dining table for some traditional-style comfort.

## HOW TO LAY A GREAT TABLE

**A wonderfully dressed table enhances the whole dining experience. When designing a setting, consider when you'll be dining (day or night), the season, the menu (type of cuisine) and who you'll be inviting. Adapt the rules of traditional table laying to embrace more creative approaches.**

- For a table with an attractive patina or finish, forget the cloth and use a runner and/or placemats instead to protect its surface and add decorative detail.

- One generous centrepiece gives the table a feeling of vitality, but it should be proportioned to allow for eye contact across the table.

- Modern style is about mixing and matching colour, texture and shape. Combine rounded forms with modern squared-off shapes, use colour as an accent against a palette of neutrals, and mix matt with more lustrous finishes.

- The table setting and food should work in harmony. Elaborate decoration works best where the food is simply presented, while busy food demands less fuss at the table.

- A night-time setting calls out for candles and mood lighting – combine these with reflective surfaces for extra sparkle.

### 1. FUSION FEAST
This rich, dark timber veneer dining table provides the backdrop for an East-meets-West decorating theme, with a casual mix of squared-off plates and bowls, chopsticks and traditional cutlery. Neutrals are accented with stylish aubergine. A centrepiece of Singapore orchids adds the final flourish.

### 2. SET THE MOOD
A table is a movable feast, where the style of dressing dictates the mood of the moment. A soft, off-white tablecloth, white tableware and stemmed glasses set a formal tone, but is made more relaxed by casual, stackable seating. Arne Jacobsen chairs from the 1950s are a key to the contemporary look, alternated here with upholstered copies for subtle variation. A small side table, preferably on castors, is a valuable extension to the dining table when entertaining.

### 3. MODERN FARMHOUSE
The scrubbed-down style of a farmhouse table adds nostalgic warmth to a room, but appears less rustic when it's teamed with modern dining chairs. With their classic Scandinavian looks, these birch and polypropylene chairs bring a contemporary feel to a traditional teak table. Drawers add to the functionality of a surface used for more than just dining: one contains office equipment and the other cutlery.

### 4. CAMOUFLAGE GEAR
A careful choice of finish and clever use of design can go a long way in reducing a coffee table's perceived bulk and size. A recessed base gives this table its floating quality, with a high-gloss epoxy finish adding to its impression of lightness.

### CHARACTER BUILDING

The mood today is less about matching and more about mixing, combining styles and textures to create something fresh. An ornate Chinese altar table or old refectory table is perfectly at ease in a contemporary setting when paired with a set of streamlined polypropylene chairs, for example. Similarly, glass-topped tables appear less cool and hard-edged when combined with the raw textures of natural woven seating. But there's an art to assembling the eclectic look – it's important to consider the compatibility of chair and table legs, as well as period styles, materials and colours.

For reassuring warmth and enduring good looks, nothing quite compares to timber for a table. It adds colour and texture through the figuring of its grain, and will inevitably anchor an all-white space. The richness of a timber such as American cherrywood or river red gum for a tabletop may be tempered with a set of brushed steel or aluminium legs.

Native Australian timbers are renowned for their depth of colour and textural variety. The majority tends towards tones of yellow or red and, where gum veins are present, the timber exudes a natural rustic quality. A rug is a useful device for separating a timber floor and table of similar tones, or unifying a contrast in colour.

Tightly grained timbers, such as cherry, rock maple, blackbutt or silver wattle, produce a table with a smooth touch and even appearance. Darker timbers, such as walnut, wenge or wood treated with a stain or lacquer, are a key element of the Asian fusion look, and are increasingly combined with glass or metal for a lighter appearance. Blond woods such as birch, rock maple and white beech, lend a Scandinavian aesthetic to simple, white-on-white decorating styles, and best serve the needs of light and spacious living.

### SETTING THE TONE

The simple decor of a contemporary-style room will often call for a table with clean lines and a mellow, lived-in feel. A new table made from salvaged timber is ideal for such a space, as are new timbers with a slightly distressed and waxed finish. Polished metal, modern laminates and glass are key to the hard-edged look of urban apartments.

Using more than three surfaces within a space creates a cluttered, unplanned look. Where it's placed within a kitchen space, a dining table with a top that mirrors the bench or cupboard surfaces will ensure an integrated feel.

The traditional farmhouse table is still a favourite for kitchens and living areas, along with tiled and stone-topped designs with wrought-iron bases.

## CHAMELEON FORMS

Table designs that can adapt to different purposes are in tune with contemporary living. Extension tables cleverly respond to fluctuating seating demands but are compact enough for everyday use. Modern extension tables are much less bulky than traditional gate leg and drop-leaf designs.

Low coffee tables can quickly convert to dining mode with tops that fold out, workbox-style, to provide an elevated surface, or legs that can be raised to the appropriate height for eating.

To ring the functional changes, tables can be built with flip tops that feature, for example, a practical Melamine on one side and a timber veneer on the other.

## SHAPE AND SIZE

For seating fewer than six people, a round table is generally more space-saving and makes for a more casual mood. A small square table also works well for intimate dining. Oval tables are another space-efficient option which, like round tables, can be easily made to accommodate extra seating. They appear less bulky than a rectangular table of equivalent proportion.

For seating more than six people, a rectangular dining table is the most practical. A table to seat six (two diners at each side and one at either end) should be 1.8 metres long; for eight, 2.2 metres long; for 10 people, 2.5 metres long.

## PLACEMENT

Where a table is placed in the centre of a room, a circular design allows a more natural flow, especially where space is tight. Allow a minimum distance of 80cm between the table's edge and the wall or adjacent furniture. For a small room, it makes sense to push the table to the wall, with bench seating on one side.

By removing some of the dining chairs and placing them around the room, the table surface is freed up for other uses, such as studying or reading, when not in full dining mode. In this way, a dining room becomes a more flexible space.

1

## CLEANING SILVER CUTLERY

**Each time you polish your silver cutlery, tiny quantities of silver are wiped away, so don't clean more often or more vigorously than is needed.**

- One of the best ways to keep your silver cutlery tarnish-free is to use it regularly and to wash it promptly afterwards. Storing cutlery in a canteen will also minimise tarnishing. Wear cotton gloves when handling silver to avoid fingermarks.

- Choose a polish that is non-abrasive. Only use products designed for silver.

- To quickly clean a quantity of silver cutlery, lay the pieces on a sheet of aluminium foil in a plastic bowl, cover with hot water and add 3 tablespoons of baking soda. Soak for 10 minutes, then rinse and dry.

- Silver dip is a powerful chemical solution that's ideal for cleaning raised or embossed details. Dip for no more than 10 seconds and rinse immediately.

- Polished cutlery should be washed before using. Wash in warm, soapy water with a soft cloth, then dry immediately. Never wash stainless steel and silver cutlery together; they react on contact to cause black spotting on the silver.

## 1. KEEP IT LOW

Low-slung furniture is the key to a spacious feel. Offering a fresh take on a credenza, this clean-lined table gains vitality from its subtle mix of materials. A white-lacquered surface topped with glass creates a neutral canvas for a 'tablescape' of carefully arranged objects. Brushed stainless-steel legs link visually to the kickboards in the adjacent kitchen, while wenge veneer adds richness and definition. The floor-hugging design gives breathing space to a series of paintings above.

## 2. FRESH COUNTRY AIR

Country style has evolved into a cleaner, less cluttered look, reflecting the greater order and efficiency demanded of busy modern lifestyles. Rush-seated ladderback chairs and a simpler, straight-legged version of the farmhouse table join other classics of the provincial look — rattan, wrought iron, toile and distressed timber — but have room to breathe in an airy, open living space.

## 3. A CAFFEINE HIT

Coffee tables can anchor a seating arrangement or act as a comfortable divide between people sitting in close quarters. A coffee table placed between facing sofas is a highly functional arrangement, and often the most space-efficient. Here, the choice of a white finish provides visual relief from the brown upholstery and timber floor, and adds a quality of lightness. A shelf saves the tabletop from becoming cluttered with books and magazines.

## 4. OTTOMAN RULE

Ottomans add style as well as functionality to interiors of any persuasion. When placed in front of a sofa, a large ottoman stands in for a coffee table, as well as serving as a footrest or extra seating. A tray is all that's needed to provide a stable, protective surface for plates and glasses. For practicality, choose upholstery that will take the knocks and spills; for a less formal look, select a different fabric to the sofa upholstery.

# BED FELLOWS

YOU SPEND ABOUT ONE-THIRD OF YOUR LIFE ASLEEP, SO YOUR BED IS A VERY IMPORTANT PIECE OF FURNITURE. MAKE IT A CENTRE FOR RELAXATION, A SPOT TO COCOON AND REJUVENATE BEFORE VENTURING OUT TO A BUSY DAY.

### 1. SLEEP AND THE CITY

Here's a good example of a modern bedroom with the right combination of elements to satisfy the tired and weary: polished floorboards, a feature wall, an upholstered fabric panel delineating the bedhead and minimal furnishings. An interesting use of different textures in the cushions and throws gives a touch of warmth. The platform bed seems to float off the floor, giving this bedroom a real designer edge.

### 2. SNOOZE IN BLUES

A young boy has the luxury of space and comfort with a double bed ensemble stylishly dressed in stripes and checks. All the bedlinen is reversible so that the room's decor can be changed at whim.

## CHOOSING A BED

You spend up to one-third of your life in bed, so it's crucial to choose one that's comfortable. If your bed is starting to sag and give you an interrupted night's sleep, it's time to invest in a new one.

As with all furniture, you do tend to get what you pay for, so don't skimp on the purchase of a new bed – spend as much as you can afford. As much as you would, say, on a top-quality sofa. After all, with a life span of around 10 years, the cost of a good bed is certain to be absorbed over time.

The most important part of the bed, in terms of snoozing, is the mattress. It should help you maintain correct posture when sleeping, so that muscles and nerves are relaxed, bone joints are unstressed, and the spine is as straight as possible.

Over the past few years, the design and manufacturing of bedding have improved greatly. New upholstery materials and better inner-spring technology have vastly upgraded coil-sprung mattresses. Soft-sided waterbeds have lost weight and look more like inner-spring ensembles, while latex mattresses offer luxurious comfort.

Generally, the more springs a mattress has, the better support it will offer. An inner-spring mattress with either pocket springs or continuous coils is a good bet. Similarly, the more padding there is, the better the prevention of pressure spots.

Many people think a firmer mattress is better, but if it's too hard it causes pressure on parts of the body and can also reduce circulation. However, it's best to err towards firmness: a soft mattress may initially feel wonderful, but will result in your shoulders and hips being out of alignment, so you'll wake stiff and achy.

## CHOOSING BEDLINEN

For most people, the important thing in choosing bedlinen is its design. And it's true; a beautifully coordinated quilt cover and sheet set or a luxurious bedspread can be a focal point in a bedroom. Changing your linen is a cheap, convenient way of changing your bedroom's overall 'look'.

What your sheets are made from affects how they wear and also how they will feel against your skin. Natural fibres such as cotton, silk and

wool have great 'breathability' and are able to withstand changes in temperature and humidity while you sleep. These are preferred by most people because they feel the most comfortable – even luxurious. Nothing quite tops the feeling of crisp, pure cotton sheets, but they do tend to wrinkle after washing. Synthetic fibres resist wrinkles and often come in brighter patterns, but they tend to stick to the skin in warm weather. One solution is to buy 'easy care' sheets, a poly-cotton blend that washes well.

Go for sheets with a high thread count – the more threads per square inch of fabric, the greater the sheet's suppleness and durability.

The best way to tell if a mattress is going to offer you the right level of comfort and support is to try it out in the store. Lie on it for a good 15 minutes (and if you share it with a partner, bring them too!). Don't be shy – your bed is an important purchase and it has to feel right. After all, people come in all shapes and sizes and what feels perfect for one person may be uncomfortable for another.

Check that the mattress still gives support when you are lying perched on the edge of the bed, and that you and your partner don't roll in towards each other.

A mattress should conform to the shape of your body. Try this test: lie on the bed flat on your back. Then slide your hand into the small of your back.

If you can't get your hand through, the mattress is too soft. If there's a gap, it's too hard. The right mattress will allow you to fit your hand through snugly. It will also 'give' a little at the pressure points of hip and shoulder when you're lying on your side.

The base of your bed is very important, too. Although there are many styles of bed around, if you are the type of person who constantly rearranges your furniture it may be worth investing in a bed on castors. This also helps with cleaning underneath it.

Remember, the foundation of your bed is as important as the mattress. While wooden slats remain popular, and these days adjustable posture slats mean you

6

### 1. CLASSIC WHITE
Classic shapes and a pale scheme produce restrained grandeur. This four-poster bed, with delicate carving atop its posts, could only be dressed in pure white linen.

### 2. MODERN LOVE
This bed's simple iron structure, with its four thin posts, offsets the trailing mosquito net beautifully. Inexpensive and functional, mosquito nets add a feel of the tropics. Note the use of white and green in this room – the clean colours contribute to an uncluttered effect.

### 3. SLEIGH RIDE
A beautiful bed needs little around it. In this room, the fantastic wooden sleigh bed is the focal point. Remember that making beds like this one can take a little more effort as the mattress is largely covered by the bed's surrounds.

### 4. BACK TO BASICS
Plain metal beds are good for smaller bedrooms or for apartment living. You can pick up beds like this at almost every major chain, but be aware that the quality does vary. Choose a bright quilt cover and hang a large artwork above the bed to make things more interesting.

### 5. STORYBOOK APPEAL
This fairytale bed comes alive with its ornate carving and handpainted finish. It's as delightful as the doll's house perched beside it. Custom-designed and handcrafted beds make a real difference in a bedroom.

### 6. MONUMENTAL
This adobe-style bedhead was fashioned from aerated concrete blocks in much the same way as a fireplace would be. It has a cute porthole feature so the owners can peek through from the washbasins which are plumbed behind it. Beaded Thai-silk cushions in chocolate and silvery tones and a faux-mink throw add glamour.

can arrange them to match the body's pressure points, for ultimate comfort it's hard to beat a proper 'ensemble' which has a foundation (also called a box-spring mattress) that acts like a shock absorber for the mattress. Experts strongly warn against putting a new mattress on an old foundation, as this can shorten a mattress's life by as much as two-thirds.

If you buy an ensemble and want the elegant look of a separate bedhead, make sure it's in proportion to the bed base and is useful as well as good-looking. It should also be solid enough to support someone leaning against it.

When it comes to size, bigger is better – a larger bed is simply more comfortable, especially if you share it with a partner and/or a pet. Most main bedrooms can accommodate a queen- or even king-size bed, so if you can afford it, upsize! You should be able to lie on a bed with your arms crossed behind your head and still feel as though you have plenty of space. The tallest occupant should also have at least 15cm between their feet and the end of the bed.

Do your research and make sure you are happy with the design and, above all, the comfort of the bed you choose, because you will have it for a long time to come. Ideally, it will provide a happy sanctuary for you to snuggle into each night – somewhere to feel warm and cocooned, and a place which revitalises you for each new day.

# BECOME A MIX MASTER

THERE IS VERY LITTLE PASSION IN A PERFECTLY COORDINATED ROOM.
MIXING IT ALL UP A BIT, INTRODUCING SOMETHING OLD TO THE NEW
AND THINKING A LITTLE LEFT OF CENTRE WILL PRODUCE A ROOM WHICH
SAYS MORE ABOUT YOUR PERSONALITY THAN YOUR BANK BALANCE.

While it's natural to want to seek harmony in your home, a totally harmonious room can be monotonous. Eclectic style is all about a look that's evolved over time, not overnight, and it takes a certain amount of courage. It includes the unexpected and the surprising. Rooms don't have to be all of one period and if there's any one rule to describe eclectism, it's in the art of the mix and the comfortable contrast.

## CREATE RHYTHM

There should be a rise and fall, a sense of rhythm in the colours, textures and shapes used through your home. Begin by establishing a favourite style, say French provincial, in one room (often it's the main bedroom). Merely hint at this style in the living room, with a decorative grouping or piece of furniture which reflects French provincial. Then add to this other design features and objects which may inspire or delight you. If you also love oriental design add something like a cabinet or screen, teak coffee table or silk cushions.

Your framed family portraits can still hang in the hall, though this contrasts nicely with your contemporary artworks in the living room. Explore the potential of an antique or two, by introducing something old and charismatic. Juxtapose very different new and old objects on a fireplace mantel or table. Add a fabulous old chair covered in a contemporary fabric. Set an antique dining table with Asian-inspired crockery. Think of elegant contrasts and inspiring design liaisons.

### 1. THE BIG PICTURE
Old doesn't have to mean antique. Junk-shop finds, even reproductions, will inject warmth. Here, a print of a classic 1920s poster brings elegance to an eclectic dining setting with a traditional refectory table and smart contemporary swivel dining chairs. A classic kilim rug gives the setting further clout.

### 2. LINK WITH COLOUR
You can use colour to integrate objects in a room, echoing an accent colour from a piece of art, for example, in a sofa. This home of an art collector includes an Italian coffee table, upholstered 1950s chairs and a Paul Klee design rug. Art pervades the indoor/outdoor living space. Remember, with large paintings it's important to be able to step back to view them properly.

## KEEP IT UNCLUTTERED

It's all too easy to view eclectic style as rooms filled with clutter or, worse, rooms which are dowdy, old-fashioned and a repository for items past their prime. But if you keep the modern goal of uncluttered space foremost in your mind, it's a cinch to incorporate traditional pieces or quirky collections without making the room feel old-fashioned. The idea is to create a light and airy home which maximises space and lets you explore the potential of your furnishings. Rooms should have visual tension and drama, but they won't if they are crowded or have sensory overload.

## USING COLOUR AND PATTERN

Painting a room white – not stark, but chalky – is a quick way to unify disparate objects so they appear more sleek and modern. But bold colours, such as ochre and oxblood, will also enhance ethnic and tribal artefacts with great shapes and textures, and certain decorative styles like Art Deco. If you don't dare paint a whole room a strong colour, limit the colour to a single wall and use this as a backdrop to a special piece of furniture or collection of fabulous things.

Using too many coloured patterns will kill the look. Yet a tribal pattern such as you'd find in African mudcloth or in a Persian rug can often be the highlight of an eclectic room – the secret here is to keep the competition in check. In a white or neutral room, you can use a multi-coloured modern rug on the floor to coordinate unmatched chairs of different periods, fabrics or timbers.

3 | 4

## 1. MOD SQUAD

Eclectic style is a clever way to decorate modest spaces. This suburban 'shed' with a shady past has been given a glorious new style with a Noguchi coffee table, Saarinen side table, Gordon Mathers chairs, an oriental blanket chest and Noguchi-inspired table lamp.

## 2. ECLECTIC EASE

Children will feel less 'stitched up' in a room where the mood is laid-back and the furnishings are not too precious. Their clutters of 'stuff' – books, toys and treasures – sit more easily in a space furnished with a mix of finishes and styles. A sofa and ottoman covered in leather are the perfect spots to stretch out and watch television for this pair of youngsters.

## 3. ROOM TO SPARE

Although a bold mix of styles creates an arresting look, it takes time and effort to get it right. In a renovated terrace, each item gains star rating against fresh white walls. It's a surprising mix: African conga drums with contemporary reproduction furniture and retro lighting – not to mention the hi-tech sound system. It's an adults-only place to prop rather than chill out.

## 4. REARRANGEMENTS

Rearranging the furniture or accessories is an easy way to refresh an eclectic room. Adding something here or there, while keeping an eye on the balance and scale of your objects, is how a scheme successfully evolves. This is a tiny room but it's been given a sense of drama with its owner's collection of black, blue and red objects.

## CARRYING THE LOAD

- Make sure a large-scale piece will fit into the intended space *before* you buy it. Measure the item and the area twice for accuracy before completing your purchase.

- Try to 'walk through' getting a large piece into your home – a turn or corner in a hallway could stop you in your tracks and that could result in a perfectly proportioned sofa (for the space) being deconstructed back at the furniture workshop and then bolted together in situ – at extra expense, of course.

- Oriental cabinets and armoires, extra-large tables, beds, televisions, hi-fi equipment and bulky items are best packed and carried by removalists. They'll take four to five hours to do a job that might take you days.

- If you have a very heavy item, like a custom-designed sandstone or formed concrete dining table, you will have to hire a piano removalist company. They use extra strong labour experienced in weight-lifting.

- Every situation is assessed individually by the removalist company. When in doubt about carrying something, don't – leave it to experienced professionals.

### TEXTURE TELLS ALL

The most obvious attraction to eclectic style is its focus on texture. This look encourages – in fact it demands – the juxtaposition of very different surfaces, like the rough with the smooth and the matt with the glossy. Take that one step further and you're likely to see concrete with silk, tile with suede, and metals with ceramic in today's sophisticated eclectic room.

Textures have an attraction similar to that of artisan-crafted furniture. You feel compelled to touch and explore the piece. Remember also that natural materials like rattan, wicker and sisal have an inviting softness which takes the hard edge off many man-made materials. These combine beautifully with old and new fabrics and furniture, becoming the tactile link between ethnic fabrics'

inherent primitiveness and the smooth surface of finely carved wooden artefacts.

### FURNITURE SHAPES

If you have a household filled with furniture, both contemporary and antique, and want to make them work together, pare back. Use minimal furnishings and carefully selected artworks or paintings. Keep the floors and walls plain (white or neutral coloured walls, plain carpet with no pronounced texture or pattern) and don't introduce patterned fabrics at all.

Combining furniture styles successfully is all about paying attention to scale and proportion, keeping in mind the sense of rhythm mentioned before. Try to keep the number of different styles to three (five if you dare); to balance this number, include at least two decorating items of a similar style or period.

Eclectic style is flexible enough to embrace many different pieces collected during your life. And done well, its verve and energy has original appeal.

Sometimes the best design solutions come through combining quirky shapes and you have to disregard whether their marriage is practical. Will the swirls in the walnut burl of a 1940s sofa table or cabinet sit comfortably in the company of sleek contemporary pottery? It's all in the relaxed balance of shapes and forms.

Details are the common bridge when you're combining pieces of different periods. Capitalise on a recurring motif. For example, if you love organic shapes, try to repeat the curve of a chair back in the design motif of a fabric, a piece of pottery or a curvy mirror. Finetune your eye to notice these things – it's important in any decorating exercise.

### 1. RHYTHM OF LIFE

It's a natural progression of every home to gather pieces from different periods. It's what you do with them that marks the difference. If you decide to furnish this way, you'll be constantly on the search for new finds – surely that's the best excuse you'll ever need to shop.

### 2. CUSTOM PIECES

There's fun to be had in the blending of old and new, creating individual looks which can't be bought off the rack. Here is a heady ensemble that's part Italian street scene, part Paris wine club. This room opens to the outside through a tilting glass door; furniture is a blend of decorator department store and custom-made items.

### 3. MAKING A CLEVER COMBINATION

Interior designers often add the clean lines of a cabinet or coffee table to a room full of antiques, but the challenge is really in placing the furniture when there is more than three or four distinctively different styles. This designer has cleverly combined Biedermeir, Art Deco, modern 1950s and more in a very chic city apartment. He's made it work by choosing pieces with similar lines and keeping the colours uniform.

### 4. DIFFERENT STROKES

Highlight the clash of antique, modern, quirky … even questionable, against a richly coloured background. This study brings together an Asian cupboard and lightweight contemporary chairs with hunting trophies. The disparate pieces are grounded by the glossy floor and coloured walls.

## SHOPPING FOR SECOND-HAND

**Buying well at auction comes down to knowing exactly what you're bidding for and how much you're willing to pay. Online auctions can be a bit riskier because you're only inspecting photographs of the items, but reputable sites have measures in place to protect buyers and sellers.**

• Vintage is just another name for second-hand. The key to successful second-hand shopping is a discerning eye. When it comes to furniture, look for either classic pieces that never date, or retro styles.

• 'Retro' refers to anything from the 1950, 1960s and 1970s. It pays to be vigilant about damage or faults – but when you can pick up a cool retro sofa that will, when re-covered, look like a million dollars, patience pays off.

• If you're buying reconditioned or second-hand whitegoods or appliances, ensure they come with a warranty.

• Always consider the source of your bargains – it pays to deal with reputable, licensed second-hand stores – and take care when buying through the classifieds.

• Remember, if it looks too good to be true, it probably is.

• Word-of-mouth is still the best way to find things. Bear in mind that vintage items in trendy shops can be just as expensive as new stuff.

## LIGHTING

You can't expect any decorating style to work if you haven't selected the correct lighting. You must be able to see the room and its furnishings clearly, but the lighting should be flexible enough for you to create the desired mood. Recessed spotlights or downlights give good overall illumination, while table lamps can help create a softer atmosphere. Use spotlights to highlight prized possessions.

## THE BEST ADVICE

The most important thing to remember is that individual taste plays a starring role in eclectic style. However, the key is in using modern elements to celebrate objects with a past, combining furnishings which give you great pleasure while adding a shot of colour and a huge dash of surprise to create the final result.

### 1. SHARE DISCOVERIES

Provided you're confident about what you like, mixing old and new is one of the most relaxed looks to achieve. It's about discoveries. Here, it's not so much the old with the new but making the traditional and classic look fresh. The room's centrepiece is the Art Nouveau-inspired, wrought-iron chandelier.

### 2. CHECKOUT CHIC

In a contemporary sense, decorating eclectically gives you the freedom to decorate the way you really want to, without following any rules. The owner of this modern townhouse enjoyed shopping at garage sales and discount stores and kept a check on furniture shops' closing days.

**3. THE FLORAL FIX**
As the art of the handmade enjoys a revival, you can be sure you'll find various interpretations in an eclectic-styled room. The distinctions between art, craft and design are perhaps less obvious in an individually styled room than in one decorated to a specific scheme. Here, the tactile nature of handmade, painted and printed fabrics works very well.

This chic living room belies
the fact that it was designed for
a young family with active boys.
Comfort is the key. The room
has an easy elegance with
highly adaptable furnishings, and
the cool biscuit, grey and
oxblood scheme shows a
wonderfully restrained hand.

An increased awareness of
family needs is coming through
in the design of living spaces
and kitchens. These once separate
zones are melding into one
multipurpose space, with the living
area often extending outdoors
to embrace nature. Alongside this
revamped social zone are indulgent
bathrooms which offer sanctuary,
and sophisticated bedrooms
with no clutter in sight. And our
preoccupation with health suggests
that spaces dedicated to gym gear
and spas are here to stay. With
home much more than a house,
decorating to suit your lifestyle is a
serious business, but it's fun, too.

# LIVING IT AND LOVING IT

LIVING ROOMS TODAY ARE LESS ABOUT FORMALITY AND MORE ABOUT COMFORT,
FLEXIBILITY AND FUN. YOU MIGHT LIKE TO MAKE A COOL STYLE STATEMENT OR
GO FOR A FUSION OF OLD AND NEW, BUT DECORATE YOUR LIVING ROOM WITH
SOOTHING COLOURS AND THE FAVOURITE THINGS YOU LOVE.

### 1. FLORAL FLAIR
When using different patterns
together, be sure to balance
them with large doses of solid
colour. Just as bright colour
tends to intimidate, big patterns
– like floral panel prints – can
overwhelm a living room.
Here, winter-pale walls are
brought to life with a vibrant
bouquet of florals, the highlight
being the charming French
panel print. What pulls the
scheme together are the plain
raspberry red sofas, dining
chairs and plush rug.

### 2. THE GREAT INDOORS
When you want the view to
be the focus, be more restrained
with the furnishings. The living
room in this coastal retreat has
enveloping views of a preserved
stand of rainforest trees. Together,
the owners and their architect
wanted to open the room as
much as possible to the dunes,
sky and trees – the result is a
'treehouse' room bounded by
large windows and sliding glass
doors. On a white beech floor,
classic woven wicker tub chairs
and futon sofas offer relaxed
seating in a great atmosphere.

The kitchen used to be the hardest
working room in the home – but not any
more. These days the living room's got
to be all things to all people, open
24 hours a day, with a floor plan and
furnishings designed to complement the
lifestyle of the modern family. With the
walls coming down on the old formal
'lounge', you have a much friendlier,
integrated kitchen/dining/living space
that allows families to spend precious
time together and gives them a bigger
place in which to entertain friends.

To cope with a modern family's needs,
there must be both quiet zones and
dedicated activity areas in the living
space. But however busy life becomes,
the living room must be able to 'shut
down' to look tranquil and tidy, and this
is where your decorating skills come into
play. Your choice of paint colours, fabrics,
flooring and furniture will reflect how
you 'feel' about your living room.

We live in unconventional times where
there are no particular design rules – only
goals. So while some people may seek
decorative refuge in minimalist spaces,
most of us still want familiar comforts in
our living rooms.

Comfort means shelter, warmth, a sense
of family and flexibility – allowing for
both seasonal change and for those changes
that come with children growing up.
But comfort also means having treasured
possessions around you – something for
you to enjoy in the company of friends.

### 1. NEW DIVISION

If you're going to knock down walls to make an open-plan space, leave some sections to create natural divisions; these can then be painted in a distinctive colour. In this waterfront home, redesigned for family-friendly living, a free-flowing space running the length of the house was created to accommodate a central kitchen with dining and living at either end. Original sofas, re-covered in a hard-wearing cotton, and a sisal rug demarcate the conversation grouping.

### 2. BORROW COLOURS

Take inspiration for the colours in your living room from a rug, a favourite fabric or from your surroundings. In this room, the colours reflect the blue of the sky and the rich red sunsets seen through the tall casement windows and doors. The French provincial-style dining table has a distressed painted finish and chairs are upholstered in a jacquard weave.

### 3. REVIVE THE PARLOUR

Traditional terrace houses have a floor plan that is long and narrow, with a hallway running the length of at least the first front room. These front rooms, originally parlours, are still ideal as sitting rooms. Even by today's standards they are a delight to decorate and a joy to relax in, if the light is right. This inspired owner has 'whitewashed' everything to define the details. Her penchant for French style is revealed with pretty accessories and innovative decorative touches.

### 4. A SPACE APART

If you have separate formal and casual living spaces, give each a distinct personality. Take stock of all the activities you want to accommodate in the formal living room. It may be only to serve as a respite from the maelstrom of family life, or be a private place to listen to music. In this room, the owners watch television while relaxing away from their children. They also entertain guests on the adjoining terrace – a sunscreen blind protects against afternoon sun.

## MODERN HABITS

Designers today take an eclectic approach when furnishing living rooms – there are contemporary interiors devised inside vintage buildings and, conversely, period features included in cutting-edge spaces.

But the important thing is to decorate to suit your individual lifestyle. Think of how you do things. Many of us don't write letters, we email. So where will you be putting your computer? If you plan your technology at the outset, you can position power points more conveniently.

Do you sit, or do you perch? Low-line furniture on legs could be preferable to big, voluptuous couches. Do you like to lounge or have a little nap before the children get home from school? A daybed might be more suitable than a sofa. And what about beanbags and squashy floor cushions? They're perfect for lounging teens who seem to gravitate to the floor.

Today, people flick more than they read, so be sure to include plenty of storage for newspapers, magazines and books. And do you graze rather than dine? If so, you'll rate a wide, low, multipurpose coffee table higher than a formal dining table.

How do you like to entertain? If you barbecue, you'll want access to the outdoors and furniture that's lightweight to easily move from indoors to out. Love having people over for dinner or cocktails? Get an extension table if you do sit-down dinners and have some spare seats on hand (think smart, stackable and lightweight) for cocktail drinkers.

Living rooms were once taboo for small children, but things are now more democratic. It's important that all your upholstered seating and soft furnishings will be able to deal with the rough stuff put out by children. Avoid over-precious upholstery. Imitation suedes, leather and washable cotton drill are perfect for active families. Remember, the style and shape of cushions, especially on sofas, can make or break the comfort factor. Try to buy soft feather-filled cushions – they'll last the distance.

### 1. PERIOD FEATURES

Sometimes renovating means reinstating not reinventing, particularly if you love period features. This also allows you to experiment with a style that's perhaps too decorative for contemporary architecture. The owner here has indulged her passion for traditional French style but uses it with modern flair. Canvas-covered sofas provide comfortable seating, with Louis XVI chairs, upholstered in their original velvet, adding authenticity. The fireplace is a new stone composite set within a traditional moulding.

### 2. DOWN TO EARTH

Introducing Mexican-style design and decorating to a home opens the door to remarkable possibilities. There's no denying the appeal of handcrafted wood, but it's the brilliant accent colours against creamy white adobe walls that win us over. The owner of this family-friendly living room, however, prefers more muted tones, and has combined earthy hues with rough timber, forged iron, wicker, leather and coir.

### 3. TRADITIONAL STYLE

Your living area doesn't need to have a contemporary look to make its connection to the outdoors. In this instance it's a contemporary home that has been given a traditional treatment. The oriental rug and sturdy wingback chair covered in a French fabric are signature elements of a classic style. They're quite at home in a room where expanses of glass have been used to create a union between indoors and out.

### 4. MAKING IT EASY

It's important to decide what you're prepared to live with before you renovate or decorate your living room. In this multipurpose living space there is none of the usual clashes about loud music, teenage friends underfoot or the beep of computer games. The secret is zoning. Each person has their own designated personal entertainment space within the house and a concealed sliding door closes off this room from the rest of the house. Smart, easy-care, suede-covered sofas are wonderful for lounging.

5

## 5. MODERN FORMAL

One of the most popular features in modern renovations is having a combined formal living and dining room and a separate, more generous family living space incorporating the kitchen. It's in these formal spaces that decorator items can be displayed with flair, and fabrics can be more 'precious'. Here, a formal dining and living space was included in the renovation of an old Californian bungalow. The French lithograph is a dominant feature tying together the warm tangerine of the suede-covered chairs with the glowing jarrah timber. Sofas are upholstered in a luxury Italian striped fabric.

## DEALING WITH OPEN PLAN

Open-plan living areas function best if you apply some designer tricks. Create separate living/working areas with back-to-back storage units or a desk butted up to a sofa. Streamline the room by building in bookcases. If the living and dining space are merged into one area, place the furniture so it doesn't impede the view across the room.

The biggest problem you eventually discover with open plan is the amplified noise and the loss of heat through large expanses of glass. The noise is not merely the clicking of high-heels on bare floorboards, but sounds coming from every corner of the room — the closing of a cupboard door, the whirring of a blender, the collapse of a pile of Lego and the noise of the television.

It's a good idea from both an acoustic and insulation point of view to put down big thick woollen rugs to absorb sound and help with warmth. Curtains and blinds at the window also cut down on heat loss and noise. Lining the walls with bookshelves (filled with books!) is another good idea for absorbing sound.

## SETTING UP A HOME BAR

**People love to eat out, but they're also dining in and entertaining at home more than ever. The home bar has come back into favour.**

You may like to set aside a part of your kitchen or living area for a home bar. Alternatively, you can build a dedicated bar complete with counter and bar stools. Check how the experts do it — it's a great excuse to visit as many wine and cocktail bars as you can to take a close look. Note the height of countertops and what they're made from (they need to be stainproof and easy to clean) and the position of foot rails and the most comfortable bar stools — with or without backs, moulded or upholstered seats, and so on. Try to have an ergonomic layout behind the bar, and allow enough bench space for preparing several drinks at once.

The basic requirements for any bar should include:

• Glasses in various sizes and shapes • Cocktail shaker and martini mixer
• Hanging racks or a cupboard for glassware • Blender • Juicer
• Storage for spirits and liqueurs • Small bar fridge for making ice, chilling wines, mixers, mineral water, etc • Sink • Dishwasher, optional but sensible • Wine rack
• Corkscrews, bottle openers and swizzle sticks • Sharp knife and cutting board
• Ice bucket • Espresso machine — the bar makes a good spot to serve coffee

### 1. DE-TOX IN STYLE

You can give your room a de-tox by choosing 'allergy-free' furnishings. After all, the living room is the most-used room in the house and everyone will benefit from a healthier atmosphere. Touch-up your senses with natural fibres and textures, as seen in this chic living room. An unusual woven wood panel is used as a room divider.

### 2. TAKE A LOW LINE

One of the most exciting elements of decorating a new apartment is being able to start with a raw canvas and build up the furnishings in layers. Here, a rich, earthy colour palette was chosen to offset a much-loved painting. The seating is modern, low and square, in line with the apartment's architectural style.

### 3. THE RIGHT WHITES

An all-white scheme is a fantastic backdrop for unusual accessories. But if you want white furniture, make sure your sofas are dressed with washable slip-covers. Here, the scheme is held together by a bold rug. To draw attention away from the low ceiling, pictures have been propped instead of hung.

## DECORATING WITH COLOUR

Colour is your secret weapon to making a living room stylish and very personal, yet it can be wasted if not used properly, particularly with open-plan living spaces.

Opt for a monochromatic scheme with a feature colour on the wall the farthest from the entrance. Then bring this feature colour forward in a sofa or accessories. Introduce splashes of this same colour in paintings or framed artworks. Or you could choose a cool colour in a plain carpet which continues the wall colour; this ploy helps blur the boundaries, highlights interesting shapes in the furniture, and lets you add richly coloured or patterned fabrics for sofas.

Your living room should contain a couple of surprise elements. Experiment by mixing original art, framed prints, handpainted ceramics or fabrics with sleek contemporary design and antiques. And don't be afraid to display your very favourite things, including your loved collections and accessories. Now that's the style of today.

## TIPS FOR SMALL-SPACE LIVING

**In a compact home, think vertical. Think integration. Think of your rooms as cubes, not squares. Push the boundaries by looking above your head and using every metre of space. The secret to getting the most out of your limited space is to make rooms dual functional or open plan.**

- Plan before you rush into knocking down walls.
- List all the activities you'll be doing in each space – don't forget entertaining, watching television and working from home – draw a plan to scale and mark zones for each activity.
- List all storage needs before you renovate or redecorate. Include space for sports gear, ironing board, travel bags and home office equipment.
- Build in furniture – it's the magic ingredient in small spaces as it de-clutters and creates a sense of openness.
- Cupboard frames and doors take up more space then open shelves. Wherever possible, use sliding doors.
- One large sofa takes up less space than two small ones.
- Go for a round table – this takes up less space than a square or rectangular one.

### 1. PURE LUXURY

Perhaps your lifestyle dictates the need for a formal living room which is used primarily for entertaining. You can then display your collectables and use a decorating style which is underscored by luxury fabrics, sumptuous seating and ornate accessories. While the style in this room is European-inspired with its Louis XVI chairs, classic table lamps and decorative mirrors, the feeling is very New York City.

### 2. COMFORT FACTOR

Some people find comfort in a room of pared-back simplicity. But here, comfort is a combination of colour and texture in a sitting room designed for lingering. Walls are painted in terracotta red with traditional toile fabric for curtains. The designer chose overscaled furniture with deep, sink-into cushions for ultimate comfort.

### 3. ANTIQUE PLEASURES

Home is a sanctuary, a place where you can close off the world and be yourself in the surrounds where you feel most comfortable. If you adore a particular decorating style or enjoy living with antiques, then go ahead and decorate with what you love. A creative couple's favourite room in their renovated cottage is this living room which is lined with French 18th-century carved panels and upright French salon chairs. This is where they entertain guests, too.

# STATE OF LIBERATION

EVERYTHING ABOUT THE NEW ATTITUDE TO ALLOCATING SPACE POINTS TO A MOVE OUTDOORS.
BLURRING THE BOUNDARIES BETWEEN INSIDE AND OUT ALLOWS EXTRA ROOM TO ENTERTAIN AND GRANTS
IMMEDIATE ACCESS TO THE GARDEN. IT'S AS IF THE LIVING ROOM HAS BEEN GENTLY EASED OUTSIDE.

What greater freedom is there than opening up your house to the garden and sky? It's acknowledging our climate and our love of the great outdoors. It's also celebrating the liberation of the house, moving it from the formally segregated series of rooms inherited from the 19th century to a series of light-filled activity zones designed to cope with a busy 21st-century agenda. When barriers are down, activities can flow from one to another – from cooking to eating to relaxing.

The importance of a home's connection with the outdoors has increased in the last 10 years. Some of the reasons for this are the occupational hazard of working increasingly longer hours indoors, the redefinition of leisure time and the need for personal respite at the end of a hectic day. A growing concern for the natural environment and an acknowledgment of the climate we live in have also helped.

This indoor/outdoor zone – whether it's a paved terrace teasing the lawn's edge, a shaded verandah or a rustic timber deck – also embodies our ability to tame and enjoy nature.

## MAKING THE CONNECTION

Some rooms are linked to the outdoors by specific materials – for example, an interior wall which projects outside and is finished in a bold textured paint or tile. For others it could be a layer of transparency – big expanses of glass which either screen or define the space. But the simplest way to merge the indoor with the out is to improve your access to the garden. For the living room and kitchen this could mean replacing a single door with french doors or even knocking out the wall entirely to create a seamless vista through wide pivoting or push-back glass panels. The whole idea is to reduce the framework so you get an uninterrupted view.

You should also consider extending the same type of floor – or at least a material of the same colour – from inside to out. Timber floorboards can give way to decking (it doesn't have to be elevated). Ceramic tile, stone and concrete can work in much the same way, for example, smooth polished concrete inside and concrete pavers outside.

## 1. STRETCHING OUT

Extending out rather than up proves a success with growing families eager to gain more bedrooms and indoor/outdoor living space. Here, a family built on another wing at the rear, with bifold kitchen windows which push back over a servery for ease when entertaining. A wall of glass opens to the paved area, literally doubling the size of the living space. Stools are weather-resistant wicker; furniture is teak.

Today, serious cooking (not just the Sunday barbecue) can be done outside in your 'outdoor room'. By extending the kitchen to the outside, it allows even the tiniest terrace or ground-floor apartment the opportunity to take on entertaining. Sometimes a kitchen bench can be extended through to the outside area to create a seamless work surface – this is ideal for serving drinks in the garden. Make sure you choose a bench surface that is impervious to weather.

Weather protection is an important consideration – you don't want to sizzle in the sun. A pergola will allow through a filtered light while a canopy or sail will shade and protect. And while it's a lovely thing to dine outdoors, some sort of structure should be used to 'close in' the setting, to give intimacy to dining areas within a large space.

## VIEWS

For spaces to come alive, there must also be a sense of progression as you move through the house to the outside, and a rise and fall of shapes and heights in the vista beyond. Keep the furniture styles sympathetic. If you want to set up a dining table and chairs in your outdoor space, choose a style that works with your living-room furniture.

Try to give perspective to the garden area by creating a focal point – something on which the eye will comfortably rest. This could be a specimen plant, a small grove of trees or flowering shrubs, a water feature, or simply a wall or fence painted in an eye-catching colour.

1

2

3

### FURNITURE TO WEATHER THE STORM

**Today, outdoor spaces are furnished with as much attention as those indoors and often require bigger bank balances. Keep in mind the following when you choose your outdoor furnishings.**

- Laminated fabrics (imitating traditional oilcloth) will stand up to the weather.
- Cotton canvas looks great outdoors but will eventually rot.
- Choose a synthetic fabric for cushions and seat covers – there's an excellent canvas substitute.
- In preference to white, opt for an 'environmental' green market umbrella. It won't discolour in the same way.
- Teak is the ideal all-climate timber for outdoor furniture, but if left untreated it will weather to a silver grey; if you don't like this, preserve it with an oil-based stain.
- Be choosy with your teak furniture – buy the very best you can afford.
- All-weather wicker looks lovely but will need to be sheltered in time.
- Also consider polypropylene, fibreglass, industrial stainless steel and wrought-iron furniture.
- Reconstituted stone is heavy but makes an excellent all-weather table.

### 1. VIEW WITH A ROOM

Traditionally, gazebos were used as breakfast rooms and sitting areas. Today, the idea of having a glassed-in room to shelter and envelop you rings of decadence. But here, atop a city penthouse apartment, it offers a window on the world while creating the ideal transition space – that zone between indoors and the great outdoors. Chairs are woven wicker; the table is fibreglass.

### 2. COURT FUNCTIONS

It's probably the intimate scale of a courtyard which makes it the ideal outdoor room, as seen in this contemporary home. Designed in two 'modules', the house has distinct formal and informal areas. But it is the connecting courtyard which offers its owners the opportunity for outdoor living and entertaining every day of the week. The space also serves as a light well, channelling sunshine into the interiors. Flooring is honed marble tile; the furniture is custom made.

### 3. TROPICAL ACCENT

Design styles transcend borders and timelines, but nowhere other than Australia do you find such interest and fascination in contemporary tropical style. Here, timber-framed pavilions influenced by Thai design are part of the renovation of an older-style cottage. Warm woods and white walls offer a wonderful backdrop to woven textures in an indoor/outdoor living space, with a blackbutt floor extending to concrete pavers.

## COLOUR SCHEMES

You can make the most of your 'outer space' by selecting colours which will draw attention to specific areas. But let's be clear about one thing: there's a colour revolution happening. Colours once used only for interiors – particularly hotter hues such as pink and purple – are now embellishing outdoor living spaces. But there is also a move towards natural colour palettes, as the colour shading of plants takes over from solid planes of colour.

An integrated colour scheme should take into account the dominant theme in your living room and embrace all the existing structures outside – the hard and soft landscaping, as well as the boundary walls, shade structures, outdoor seating, pots and statuary.

## WATER FEATURES

The look and sound of trickling water is both cooling and relaxing and it provides a most engaging focal point in the garden. A water feature could be as simple as a water-filled glazed urn tucked into the garden, or as complex as a waterfall over a stainless-steel sculpture.

A lap or plunge pool can be designed to cross the interior boundary, coming inside to double the potential of your entertaining space. But there are safety regulations to consider if you are planning this type of design. Check with your local council.

## LIGHTING

When you plan your garden, you should be thinking about lighting, too. Subtle lighting is better for dining by, while stronger task lighting is appropriate for traffic areas. It's better not to see the light fittings – only the light they throw. Use up-lights, where possible, as they give a more attractive effect.

In the long term, the 'outdoor room' will become a fixture in residential design; as important as the integrated kitchen and family area, or the 'day spa' bathroom of today.

### 1. OPEN UP

A lanai is an open-sided room which allows you to enjoy garden views while being protected from the sun and cold breezes. Here, the architect has designed the perfect playroom for relaxing and entertaining around the adjoining swimming pool. This cool retreat provides a year-round chill-out zone for family and friends. Flooring is concrete pavers; furniture is tallowwood.

### 2. CITY-STYLE DECK

Timber decks were once only associated with the suburbs, but here it has a more urban feel. The owner loves to entertain and uses his new outdoor area, with its sculptural woven wicker seating, like another room. He built the jarrah timber deck on the northern side of the house so he and his guests could enjoy leisurely lunches in sunshine filtered by a leafy tree. An adjacent outdoor shower is positioned in a screened nook. The dining table is custom made and lightweight designer chairs are easily stacked away when not in use.

### 3. JUST RELAX

You can create a special place for relaxation on a porch or covered deck. Whether at the front or back of a house, it has its own delightful charm. Here, pretty lemon-painted weatherboards are offset by natural timber decking. Contemporary touches, like the stylish furniture, bring the house into today.

### 4. MAKE IT VERSATILE

A shaded structure is important for children who love to play in both sunshine and rain. It's also a great destination for elegant parties and family lunches. Be sure you have a flat surface for your dining table and chairs and select a durable flooring material like concrete or stone pavers – something that'll take the wear and tear of constant traffic, oil and wine spills.

## COLOURS THAT COMPLEMENT PLANTS

**Modern-day living is increasingly moving from indoor spaces to gardens, decks and courtyards. Make the most of your integrated space.**

- Use plants in combination with paint colours to create the outdoor palette.
- No colour works better than a bright purply-blue for highlighting the depth, gloss and texture of foliage.
- If you have used red indoors, repeat it outdoors in flowers. Red is green's natural complement and the result will be well balanced.
- Use colours which harmonise inside and out. Avoid strong contrasts.
- Paint different walls in your garden area in terracotta, sienna and ochre and pick up these colours in your living room with the fabric on sofas and cushions.
- White makes a great combination with green and it seems to leap out at twilight.
- The eye picks up blue best in the early evening, so plant your blue flowers in semi-shaded areas of the garden.
- A sophisticated urban palette of soft grey, charcoal and stark white highlights the gloss and texture of greenery.

**I. PARTY NIBBLES**
The kitchen is the new entertaining space – a place where friends and family gather in an informal fashion. This kitchen, in an apartment that's nestled right beside the water, was renovated to maximise the indoor/outdoor concept and opened to the living room. The owners gather here to relax and entertain. A red-baize pool table is a star attraction.

# KITCHEN CONFIDENTIAL

THE KITCHEN HAS BEEN LIBERATED FROM ISOLATION TO BE INTEGRATED INTO THE LIVING ROOM. QUITE LITERALLY, THE WALLS HAVE COME DOWN.

The kitchen is the new playroom and entertaining space; it's where you prepare for the day and often end it. Chat room and nerve centre, the kitchen has absorbed so many roles that it's redefined the way you use the space.

But this new focus on kitchen living doesn't mean that you can neglect its principal function as a meals preparation area – it must be somewhere you can cook. Many domestic kitchens have borrowed the look of the professional kitchen, with sleek stainless-steel benches and appliances a popular choice.

Sound planning becomes even more critical when the kitchen is integrated into a living area. An island bench, for example, may also do service as the family dining table. Kitchen storage has become an art form – drawers and cupboards for every need, including sophisticated pantries and places for wine, are hidden from the eye only to reveal their contents – as if by magic – when gently touched or pulled.

Borrowing heavily from the science lab, the design of the kitchen sink has gone full circle – except that today it's bigger and deeper. And in a move away from the traditional tiled splashback, toughened glass has arrived on the kitchen scene with vast expanses, colour-backed to choice, rising above the steamy cooktop, sometimes to the ceiling.

The laundry has expanded as it relocates from the kitchen and bathroom back to a space of its own. But for some people it's all but disappeared, shrunk to a space within a traffic zone camouflaged behind a stylish fabric blind or built-in storage.

**2. WINE AT HAND**
Wine enthusiasts will savour the prospect of having their collection somewhere easy to access. The decision to include a wine rack in an open-plan kitchen should be based on how often you drink wine. Unless you're serious about your wine, it's an unnecessary inclusion. A feature of this kitchen is the sculptural metal wine rack designed as a dividing device, affording privacy to the living area while maintaining an association with entertaining.

## SAFETY IN THE KITCHEN AND LAUNDRY

**There are commonsense things you can do to make accidents less likely – just keeping heavy or sharp objects like knives out of a toddler's reach is a start.**

- Keep tiny tots out of kitchen cupboards, fridges and ovens with angle locks on drawers and doors.
- Make sure mobile storage units have lockable castors to keep them secure.
- Install a smoke alarm near the kitchen – but not too close or it may be set off every time you burn the toast.
- Store a fire blanket in a drawer for quick access – a blanket is the best way to put out a kitchen blaze in a hurry.
- Make sure laundry cupboards can't be opened by children. If cupboard or dryer doors are at ground level, secure them with a lock or multipurpose adhesive latch.
- Safety experts recommend you install a dry-powder fire extinguisher in the laundry for use on emergency fires around the house.

### 1. DON'T OVERDO IT

Too many materials, finishes and colours in the kitchen can over-complicate things, so if a surface works and it looks good, stick with it. But remember, too, budget always plays a big role in determining your benchtop. In this kitchen, the priorities were for a light-reflecting, tough yet glamorous work surface for owners who rarely cook. They chose an aqua resin material which has the appearance of glass.

### 2. APPROACHING THE BENCH

The benchtop gives the kitchen its signature and should be one of the first things selected. Concrete has made its way into the kitchen, first as flooring and then as a hard-wearing work surface. The benchtop in this kitchen has the look of concrete but the effect is from a special painted finish – it also resembles zinc with its greyer, pewter-like seductive sheen.

### 3. ADAPT A STYLE

Today's kitchen is not one lifted from a manufacturer's brochure, nor is it the same as your neighbour's. The picture that emerges is one of individuality. Even if you love a particular style, such as French provincial, you can modify it to suit your personal tastes, as the owner of this kitchen has done. It features in an all-white house, yet the mood significantly changes with joinery painted with a soft french wash.

## CHOOSING KITCHEN KNIVES

**When buying knives, check the following.**

- Make sure the knife is comfortable and balanced and feels good in your hand. Its handle should be form-fitting and made from a non-porous material.
- Just because a knife set is 'branded' by a chef, it doesn't mean it's the right one for you.
- Buy the very best kitchen knives that you can afford.
- The best knives are constructed with a full tang (the portion of the blade which fits inside the handle) running the length of the handle. You can see this if you look at the knife on its edge. If the tang doesn't go through the handle, the knife is of lesser quality.
- There are two knives that you should never be without – the chef's knife and a paring knife.
- Always keep your knives sharpened.
- The best knives are made from high-carbon surgical stainless steel.
- Except for bread knives, avoid serrated edged knives – they can't be sharpened.
- Make sure the knife block stores each knife horizontally not vertically. Vertical slots will blunt the blade unless the knife is always inserted with its sharp side up.

### 1. ZONING IN

A strategic use of colour can highlight different zones in an open-plan kitchen. A multipurpose space will certainly benefit from visual markers like a panel of coloured glass or mosaic tile. Here, the designer has made allocation for a 'formal' dining area on the far side of the kitchen bench, identified by a wall painted in deep lime, with a pretty table setting coordinated to match.

### 2. KITCHEN DRAMA

Safe and sensible whites and neutrals can be pushed aside in preference to colour, pattern and drama. Decoration can be an intrinsic part of the structure of the kitchen. In this 21st-century revival of a Gothic church, the kitchen is the focal point of the living area. The island bench is made from Castlemaine slate and recycled baltic pine, with cabinetry constructed in hardwood.

### 3. CHEFS ON SHOW

The integrated kitchen can present somewhat of a challenge if the cook is a shy performer or if you discover the sound of the dishwasher drowns out the television. This style of kitchen is where everyone is welcome, except a messy cook, so take some care in determining your lifestyle before embarking on an inclusive 'kitchen in a cupboard' style.

3

### 1. NURTURE NATURE

The kitchen's association with nurturing has never been stronger. It's here you connect with other people by having a cup of tea or preparing meals, and you also connect to that other rejuvenating part of the home – the outdoors. In this kitchen, an upholstered seat has been boxed into a picture window, and the owner can enjoy her baby while soaking up the morning sun.

### 2. THINK ECLECTIC

You can still have the latest appliances in a kitchen which combines old and new. The owner of this kitchen removed a wall to link the kitchen with the indoor/outdoor living space. A single bank of timber veneer cabinets houses the appliances, and an old solid jarrah chemistry lab table has been converted into an island bench to hold kitchen gear. Food is prepared in the larder concealed behind a sliding door.

### 3. BRIGHT IDEAS

Using laminates and glossy polyurethane finishes are a great way to introduce colour to a kitchen. The polyurethane treatment is available in most paint colours. Laminate's image in recent years has been hiked up due to the infinite array of colours, textures and patterns on offer. The designer of this kitchen draws attention to the free-form bench by combining brilliant colour with textured wood and patterned granite.

### MUST-HAVES FOR A MODERN COOK

**To cook and eat well, you need only a few items, but go for quality. This list will get you started.**

- Wok (for quick and easy stir-fries)
- Wok spoon
- Large pot (for cooking pasta)
- Pan (large enough to cook pasta sauce for two)
- Colander
- Wooden spoon
- Chopping board
- Very sharp knife
- Heavy baking tray
- Small omelette pan

With these kitchen staples, you can whip up simple stir-fries, endless pasta dishes, delicious omelettes and prepare tasty roasts with minimum effort.

### 1. FULL WASH CYCLE

If you have a large family you'll be washing almost daily, so it's sensible to have a separate laundry well away from the kitchen and with access to an outside drying area. A room dedicated to laundry helps a home work like a well-oiled machine. This laundry is in the home of a business couple and their two small girls. A hanging rail was imperative to drip-dry work shirts. Twin dryers and two washing machines were installed to save on the waiting time for fresh clothes.

### 2. FITTING IT IN

When you are buying an apartment or townhouse off the plan, make sure you are satisfied that the laundry facilities are up to your demands. Located in a large, open-plan townhouse, this laundry space does the trick for a busy couple. When not in use, the washer and dryer are neatly concealed behind a stylish roller blind. Rather than stacking the appliances, you can stagger them like the owners have done here, creating more practical storage space for the clothes basket and freshly folded clothes. Note, too, how the old laundry sink has given way to a smart porcelain tank or canal-shaped vessel with a slimline mixer tap.

### 3. BEHIND THE DOORS

Decorating a laundry is often an afterthought, but if it's somewhere you'll spend time each day, consider a scheme that's calm, relaxing and low-maintenance. Off-white or cream is less tiring on the eye than stark white, and stainless steel is a good all-rounder. Here, the owner wanted his house to look like an apartment and didn't need a large laundry space, so he designed his laundry as an extension of the L-shaped open-plan kitchen. The appliances are camouflaged behind cupboard doors. The floor is sealed limestone and there's a drying court through the rear sliding doors.

### 4. ALL IN ORDER

When space is at a premium, go for a laundry in a cupboard. Ideally, this suits a kitchen which has direct access to the garden and clothes line. Laundry and food preparation don't mix well, so position your laundry facilities away from the work area of a kitchen. Here, hidden from view behind smooth white semi-gloss lacquered cupboards in a corridor leading to the bedrooms, is a laundry with front-loading washer stacked with a dryer. Also disguised is a tiled area for drip-drying clothes and a small trough for hand-washing.

### 1. ADOBE STYLE

Hard edges and highly polished surfaces have no place in this Mexican-inspired ensuite. Instead, the walls and the spa surround are gently curved in the adobe style, built of rounded Hebel blocks and painted white. A natural palette of timber and earthy ceramic tiles breathes warmth into the room. A rush-seated stool, bamboo ladder (used as a towel rail) and hand-thrown pots add to the raw appeal of this simple, sanctuary-like space.

### 2. LOVING THE TUB

The freestanding roll-top bath is a perennial favourite for a bathroom. With most fittings arranged around a room's perimeter, it can solve the problem of having an 'empty middle' to the bathroom. This bath is the star of an airy white ensemble. Positioned for enjoying views of the garden through glazed double doors, the bath forms a natural focal point, with other fittings kept simple so as not to detract from its celebrity status. A mobile storage unit helps keep towels and bath products within easy reach of the bather.

# MAKE BATHROOMS BLISS

THE PURELY FUNCTIONAL WASHROOM HAS BECOME A SENSUAL CENTRE OF THE HOME. YOU SHOULD BE ABLE TO LEAVE THE BATHROOM REFRESHED AND HAPPY AND READY TO FACE THE WORLD.

Bathrooms today are places devoted to relaxation, rejuvenation and wellbeing. More thought, care and budget is being lavished on these hardworking spaces to make them pleasurable environments to chill out and de-stress, but they must still be able to meet the demands of a hectic morning schedule.

### REDEFINING THE BATHROOM

Boundaries between the bedroom and bathroom are becoming increasingly blurred. Sometimes there is no division at all, so bathroom fittings must be elegant enough to stay out on show. Bathroom cabinetry as sophisticated as fine furniture is no longer unusual. Often these spaces are also wired for sound or television to help get you in 'relax' mode.

With laundry facilities now frequently located in the kitchen or back in their own room, it means that a corner of the bathroom could be devoted to a small gym or exercise space, instead of holding the washer and dryer.

Meeting these varied functions in an often tight space, while dealing with the plumbing and other requirements, makes the bathroom a challenging space to plan. Clearance areas around major fittings and their relationship to features such as windows and doors need to be taken into account when designing a floor plan.

Other design decisions are dictated by how a bathroom is to be used. What's required in a family bathroom is quite different to the essentials of an ensuite. These factors will affect what sort of

storage is included, the choice of single or twin basins, double or single showers, whether a bath is a priority, and so on.

### THE NEW LOOK FOR FITTINGS

New shapes and materials are changing the appearance of bathrooms, with inspiration being sought from diverse sources – from the traditional Japanese bathhouse with its deep cedar baths to temple-like Balinese spas, from luxurious hotel suites to the clean-cut purity of industrial-inspired design.

Basins have morphed into vessels that rest on top of a vanity rather than being set into a bench, or form elongated planes in materials such as stainless steel, textured glass, Corian and marine-grade timber, as well as vitrified porcelain.

2

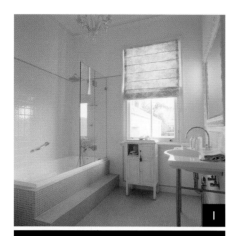

## DRAWING A GREAT BATH

In these days of fast showers and time-critical morning routines, it's easy to overlook the benefits of taking a bath. Yet soaking away the stresses and strains of a busy day is one of life's simple pleasures. Bathing in a warm bath can promote deep relaxation and sound sleep, soothe skin disorders and ease aches and pains.

Create the right mood for pampering by placing lighted candles around the tub and playing your favourite music, and set aside an hour of uninterrupted time. Add your favourite bath product or a few drops of soothing essential oils to the running water. Lavender (3 drops), bergamot (2 drops) and marjoram (1 drop) in 1 tablespoon of almond oil will help calm your mind, fill the room with fragrance and leave your skin feeling soft.

The bath water should be at a temperature that is comfortable for you, but hot enough to promote a sense of deep relaxation.

Indulge in scented soaps and body scrubs, and have your bathrobe and plenty of fluffy towels at hand to wrap yourself in. Vases of flowers, foot-friendly bath mats and plush flannels and towels can all give your home bathroom the pampering feel of a luxurious health spa.

Taps have become more sleek and sculptural. Advances in technology have given birth to baths made entirely of glass or curved, frameless glass shower screens. At the other extreme, salvaged antique bathware can be teamed with simple modern pieces to bring a sense of nostalgia without slavishly following a period look.

In contemporary bathrooms, smooth surfaces, pared-back fittings and a feeling of openness induce a sense of calm.

Finishes on the walls and floors dictate the ambience and overall colour scheme of a bathroom. White, while traditionally associated with cleanliness, is now often chosen to create a mood of simplicity and calm; a neutral palette has the same effect.

A white scheme is also immune to the whims of fashion – an important consideration in the bathroom, where changing the colour of the walls often means expensive re-tiling and not just a simple paint job. Individuality comes from the choice of coloured towels, soaps and other accessories.

Taps and shower fittings are key elements in a bathroom's style, and can be easily updated to refresh an existing fit-out. To keep things from looking cluttered or confused, extend the same design and finish to other metal fittings such as towel rails and toilet-roll holders.

### A LITTLE INDULGENCE

Spa baths, while very relaxing, take up a sizeable chunk of a room and can visually overwhelm a space, so many people are opting for hi-tech showers with massaging jets for relaxing or invigorating the body. But the ultimate concession to indulgence must be a bathroom with heated floors or a fireplace purely for sensory pleasure.

### 1. OLD WITH NEW

This cool green and white bathroom is feminine without being fussy. An antique cupboard, toile de Jouy blind and crystal chandelier are key ingredients for a look that's nostalgic but not old-fashioned. Contemporary fittings, such as a swan-neck spout and frameless glass shower screen, add a light touch without compromising the room's period feel. Remember, fabric in a bathroom risks becoming limp and mildewed unless there is good ventilation in the room.

### 2. KEEPING IT SIMPLE

An all-white approach works well in any style of bathroom. Touches of colour can come from towels, soaps, flowers or a leafy view. A large double-hung window brings the outdoors in to this room, and a glass-brick wall draws in natural light while safeguarding privacy for the toilet and shower area. The half-wall divides the space for greater intimacy and provides hanging space for towels. A single row of shell relief tiles and a naked branch in a vase are all the decoration needed.

### 3. A POLISHED VENEER

These days, bathroom vanities look no different from the furniture found in living rooms or bedrooms. Where timber veneers are used, they must be sealed to protect against the effects of water. Here, a walnut vanity is fitted with vessel basins in stainless steel. The long, ceiling-mounted tap was installed with an aerator to prevent the water splashing when it hits the basin.

### 4. OFF THE FLOOR

Keeping the floor clear adds a sense of space to small rooms. Here, white fittings blend into the walls and a wall-hung vanity and toilet enhance the air of spaciousness. The concealed cistern also creates a useful shelf space. White fittings and walls combine with touches of black in the porcelain vanity top and the tiles. Laying the large square tiles on an angle also visually 'pushes out' the walls.

### 1. PERFECT FINISHES

Design and detailing are deliberately kept simple to highlight the quality of the finishes in this luxurious penthouse bathroom. Walls, floors and vanity are lined in Carrara marble, creating a look that's strongly integrated and streamlined, with subtle decoration provided by the stone's natural veining. Mirrored surfaces reflect skyline views and bounce natural light around the space. Vessel-shaped basins in frosted glass are like sculptures.

### 2. ACHIEVE A BALANCE

Breaking with convention to overcome the limitations of a confined space, this shower has been designed on a circular footprint and fitted with a curved acrylic screen. A frosted section ensures privacy without compromising the flow of light. A glass vessel basin set on a white marble benchtop continues the lightness of touch. As part of the contemporary aesthetic for revealing the structure of an object, the basin's plumbing is left exposed rather than boxed in, avoiding unnecessary visual bulk. Cabinets in wenge veneer and slate-green mosaic tiles in the shower area balance the lighter finishes.

### 3. WELL FURNISHED

For a look that's crisp, clean and classic, you can't go past black and white, and this is a popular choice for hotel-inspired bathrooms. Here, an unfitted vanity bench is painted in a black satin finish. Twin lamps flank the unusually shaped ceramic basin, creating a more 'furnished' look.

### 4. FOR THE FAMILY

Blue is perennially popular for a bathroom, being the colour associated with water. Matt-finish, blue-green ceramic tiles line the floor of this room and form a splashback which continues as a stripe along the walls. Plenty of natural light prevents the blues from appearing cold. A step up to the bath provides a place to perch while bathing children and makes for an easier entry and exit. A nib wall screens the toilet from general view.

### 5. GRANITE FACED

Durable and naturally impervious to water, granite is a practical as well as beautiful choice for a bathroom. Here, light and dark granite tiles and cherrywood cabinetry create a strongly masculine look for a gentleman's ensuite. A curved glass shower screen minimises intrusion within the space. The low ceiling height, typical of many bathrooms, makes recessed lighting the obvious choice here.

### 6. ILLUSIONS OF SPACE

Choose finishes that are highly reflective, like mirror, to help open up a tight space, such as in this bathroom. A glass benchtop sitting on steel rods appears to float above a charcoal-grey laminate vanity, preventing it appearing too solid and heavy. To reduce the room's perceived height, the ceiling and upper wall section have been painted the same dark smoky-grey as the vanity, making the ceiling appear lower for a more intimate feel.

## CLEANING GLASS

Shower screens, vanity tops, splashbacks, vessel-shaped basins, even baths are increasingly being formed from durable glass. To maintain its good looks, glass demands regular cleaning, though 'self-cleaning glass' is said to reduce cleaning time by up to 90 per cent, thanks to a super-smooth finish that prevents dirt becoming trapped. Acid-etched glass is generally less prone to soiling than sandblasted glass, which is more porous and liable to be fingermarked. Never use abrasive cleaners or scouring pads on glass, and avoid powder-based cleaners. A simple, environmentally-sound cleaning solution can be made by dissolving 20ml lavender oil in 10ml methylated spirits. Apply with a soft, damp, lint-free cloth, then buff off with wads of newspaper. For small areas of stubborn soap build-up, gently wipe with a paste of salt and lemon juice, being careful not to scratch the surface of the glass. Good ventilation and effective steam extraction will prevent mirrors from becoming fogged and keep surfaces mould-free. Heating elements at the back of mirrors will also keep steam at bay.

### 1. TAKE IT EASY
Setting the right mood for relaxation is important in your home day spa – it lifts a bathroom out of its everyday functionality. This corner spa bath has a wide surround; the perfect place for scented candles or maybe a glass of bubbly. A curve of windows, dressed with venetian blinds, allows in diffused sunlight while preserving the bather's privacy.

# PHYSICAL PLEASURES

A HOME GYM WORKS THE MUSCLES AND A HOME DAY SPA SOOTHES BODY AND SOUL.

Your mind and body need work and play, activity and relaxation in equal doses. Having a home gym where you can sculpt your muscles or a day spa-inspired bathroom where you can rest in bliss is undoubtedly indulgent, but wouldn't a little luxury give your whole life a more positive spin? Feeling good about yourself is today's mantra.

Of course the equipment for a spa and gym take space. Serenity and a perfect pedicure can be achieved in a bathroom which is not much bigger than a cupboard, but gym equipment works best if you're not crunching your elbows along with your abs – space is crucial.

Take your pursuit of physical pleasure seriously. Plan a zone to include room for gym gear, a spa bath or a spot to sit and unwind. Give yourself a view, plenty of natural light and fresh air. It's time to invest in having a good time.

### 2. ROOM FOR TWO
Bathing with a loved one is a sweet indulgence. This bath area is at one end of a bedroom, so its occupants have their own world of washing, soaking and sleeping. As well as the double spa bath, there's a large shower with a standard and a massage shower head and body jets from the side walls.

1

## HOME GYM ESSENTIALS

**BEING MOTIVATED** is the most important thing for exercise. Set up your home gym somewhere that's pleasant to be — that way you'll want to go there. Avoid garages, sheds and dark places. A television on the wall and music to listen to also makes training more fun.
**SPACE** for equipment and an uncluttered floor where you can move around easily is a must. A treadmill with an incline and most multistations need a minimum ceiling height of 2.4 metres.
**FLOORS** must be solid enough to take the weight of equipment. Place rubber mats under the gear to protect the floor and provide some sound insulation. If you are using free weights, put the rubber mat under the bench or area where you'll be lifting the weights.
**ROOM TEMPERATURE** should sit between 18°C to 22°C. You'll be working up a sweat, so having fresh air circulating will cool you down. Air-conditioning is very useful, too.
**NATURAL LIGHT** is best, and an opening window also lets in a breeze. Avoid having halogen lights in a home gym as they can heat up an area; cool-running fluorescents are better.

### 1. BREATHE EASY

Bathrooms are bigger than ever. A shower where you can spread out your arms and enough floor space to do stretches or just sit and meditate make for an indulgent experience. This room has an open-ended shower screened by a single glass panel, and its limestone tiled floor slopes to a wide grate; the wall is finished with limestone strips. A long bench opposite easily fits two basins. An African stool offers a place to rest, and a low-set window allows for cross-ventilation and extra sunshine.

## 2. THE BEAUTY STORE

Having generous space to store cosmetics and toiletries banishes clutter and streamlines the decor. This private beautician's studio, in a huge new home, has storage to spare. Honeyed tones in the ceramic tiles and timber give a warm look, making it a more appealing spot to have a massage. A hairdresser's basin, complete with pull-out rinsing spray, and an evenly lit span of mirror set the mood.

## 3. A WELCOMING GYM

The first rule of any gym should be that it's somewhere you're happy to be. Sunlight, good cross-ventilation and plenty of room to move make a most attractive place to exercise. Here there's even a television mounted on the ceiling – just like at professional gyms – so the owners can work out while watching their favourite shows. Gyms should not be too hot or too cold, so here louvres and vertical drapes are used to tame the temperature. It's illuminated by a cool-running fluorescent fitting to avoid any extra heat from the lights.

## 4. IN EASY REACH

Giving yourself a facial is a simple indulgence when everything you need is literally within hand's reach. This lavishly large square basin makes the beauty routine a pleasure. The bath-style soap rack, useful ledge and towel rail beneath the basin look stylish but are also very practical inclusions. Polished marble on the wall ups the luxe, but be sure that any stone you use in the bathroom is well sealed. Porous materials, such as marble, will absorb oil from spilled cosmetics and stain if not properly protected.

## 5. ADDING BUBBLES

Including a spa bath puts any bathroom into the comfort zone. Just remember that when it's full of water, a spa bath can weigh around 300kg, so make sure the bathroom floor is up to it. You'll also need space to install the spa pump. In this room, a penthouse view over the coast epitomises luxury; both the spa bath and shower are positioned so their occupant can take in the glorious scene.

### 1.&2. HIDEAWAY OPTIONS
The neatest way to integrate a home office into another room is to keep it in a cupboard. Be sure to give the equipment space to breathe to prevent it overheating. This built-in arrangement sits right next to the kitchen in a family-friendly living area. The shelves are adjustable to accommodate different equipment, and the keyboards (both musical and computer) sit on pull-out shelves. Bifold doors can be pulled across to tidy everything away. A desk with phone and fax facilities has been built in another corner.

# THE INSIDE JOB

THE HOME OFFICE CAN BE A FULLY FLEDGED WORK SPACE OR A NEAT LITTLE CORNER WHERE YOU DO HOUSEHOLD ACCOUNTS. BUT WHATEVER ITS SIZE, EQUIP IT WITH STORAGE, GOOD LIGHT AND A PROPER CHAIR.

A SOHO (small office home office) is part of the modern home, even if it's just a desk and a computer. If you and your family use a computer mainly for emails, schoolwork and fun, it's all right to have it in a corner of the living/dining space. But if your home office is where you earn a living, you'll want more noise control. Choose a spot away from the household traffic so you can get the quiet you need. If you have clients visiting, it's best if your office has a separate entrance, or at least a direct route from the front door.

You can be more creative with colour in your home workspace. Yellow brings a sense of energy and sunshine and reds and softer orange tones — think ochre and terracotta rather than acid orange — are warm and welcoming. Blues and lavenders are calming and a good choice if your work involves a lot of detail and concentration. Stronger blues, contrasted with white, give a feeling of efficiency. But if you're into mellow moods, team natural tones and neutrals for a sense of harmony and balance.

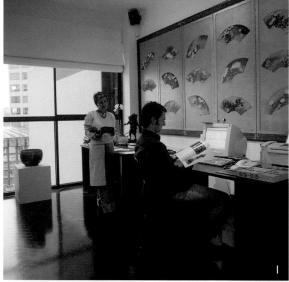

### 1. GRAPHIC ARTS

An antique Japanese screen and beautiful herringbone parquetry floor add elegance to this Melbourne home-cum-gallery. The black desks, which in another setting could have looked fairly pedestrian, take on a graphic quality when positioned against the decorative floor and artworks. A wall of windows pulls in the sunlight, so the computer is placed side-on to the glazing to avoid glare and reflections falling on the screen.

### 2. STRIKING A BALANCE

When your work and play spaces combine, you must strike a balance between colours that energise and those which calm. The easiest solution is a white or neutral background, with a potent accent colour used in furnishings to zap up the mood. In this apartment, a trestle table and mobile drawer unit make up the work area; opposite is a luscious red sofa which is very useful as a chill-out zone.

### 3. CLOSE THE DOOR

A freestanding, red-painted cupboard conceals a mini office in this living room. A computer settles on one shelf, with the printer on the shelf above. Below is a pull-out storage unit with space for hanging files and a basket for office paraphernalia. Bifold doors on the cupboard don't intrude too far into the room when opened, and when work is done, the doors are closed and the 'office' is hidden away.

### 4. BEYOND THE GREY

Corporate colour clichés can be happily forgotten in the SOHO. Choose hues which energise your mood and make you feel good. A yellow-toned ochre wall makes for a softer, more welcoming space – something to think about if you have clients visiting. And with older CRT-style computer screens being replaced by laptops and LCD flatscreens, there is more choice about where to place your computer. As well as the screens being smaller, there's no need to worry about radiation from their backs bathing visitors in an unhealthy glow.

## 5. TOP SHELF

'You can never have enough storage' could well be the SOHO mantra. But that doesn't restrict you to banks of dull grey filing cabinets. Custom-built storage using cabinet timbers such as walnut and maple gives a home office clout – just make sure there's enough space for what you need now and for the next 10 years. Remember, roll-out storage units can also double as an extra work surface. Allocating enough power points and data points for equipment will make your life easier, too.

### KEEPING IT ORGANISED

**It's easy to suffocate under blizzards of paper. Here's how to keep the decks clear.**

- Binge on storage. Cupboards and shelves can be built right to the ceiling – even over doors and windows – to make the most of wall space. You can also use wall-mounted filing trays and storage that clips under a shelf to free up a cramped desk.
- Get a good filing system. Use a filing cabinet, expanding file or a drawer to hold all your papers. Create useful folders: bills to pay, warranties, prescriptions, etc. File or bin your bits of paper as soon as you've read them, then go through the files every six months and do a cull.
- Tidy as you go. Put things away into their designated space immediately after you use them; that way you'll never be scrabbling for a pen, sticky notes or a stapler.
- Tame those cables. As well as looking messy, a spaghetti of leads attracts dust. Run them in tracks on top of skirting boards and coil the slack, or have cabling ducts recessed into the ceiling or wall. Or reduce the problem by going for wireless connections whenever you can.
- Finally, close the door. Hiding clutter behind a cupboard door is the quickest way to tidy up.

### 1. UP IN THE ATTIC

Converting an attic room or a garage can be a convenient solution when you need a separate workroom. But get the basics like insulation right – you don't want to be too hot or cold. Built-in shelves and a wall-mounted bench get around the problem of the sloping walls in this attic room; standard furnishings would have been an awkward fit. A simple blind helps control the sunshine and an anglepoise light takes care of task lighting. Budget-savvy white finishes visually expand the small space, while funky desk chairs give a spark of colour.

### 2. PLENTY OF SPACE

Shelves that go to the ceiling and a desk that seems to stretch forever make for a supremely functional work area. Not enough space is a common bugbear for home-office users, but here there's plenty of room to spread and grow, with yet another workbench positioned beside the desk under a louvred window. The walls have been given a textured finish which borrows its colour from the clouds – a good choice which amplifies the light in this downstairs room. And ergonomics aren't forgotten with an adjustable chair on a swivel-castor base.

### 3. HIDE THE COMPUTER

Computers, printers and other office gear aren't always lovely to look at, and this becomes a problem when they're on show in the living area. Instead of staring at a computer tower, give it a home behind a cupboard door – but don't forget about the computer cables connecting to the screen. The storage unit shown here swallows a mound of office clutter, as well as holding speakers for a home-theatre system on its top shelves.

### 4. FRESH IDEAS

A home office can be incorporated in a casual living space, especially when the computer is used by all the family. This creative couple – he's a ceramicist, she's a fashion designer – blend work and family in their home. This light-flooded room is inspiring to work in. Fresh air and sunlight keep the mind bright, and a home office that enjoys both is sure to be a productive place.

## SOHO ESSENTIALS

- A desk 68-73cm high, 75-85cm deep and 120-140cm wide to fit a phone and a desktop computer (if you use one). Allow 85cm behind your chair so you can get in and out.
- A good chair for back support. It should adjust up and down, backwards and forwards and have a swivel seat. When you sit at a computer, your thighs should be horizontal (shorter people should have a footrest), elbows should be bent at 90 degrees, and you should be looking straight ahead at the middle of the screen.
- Adequate lighting to avoid eyestrain. You'll need at least 100 watts where walls and ceilings are in a light colour, more if they're darker or timber panelled. An adjustable desk lamp is best for task lighting; a fluorescent globe produces less heat than an incandescent one.
- Good ventilation and sunshine to keep your brain sparking through the day.
- Enough power points and data points for all your equipment. Piggybacking power plugs is a big no-no, so invest in some powerboards.
- Shelves and a filing cabinet for easy access to papers.
- If you have clients visiting, a place for them to sit.

I

# THE SLEEP CENTRE

THE BEDROOM IS WHERE YOU INDULGE YOUR OWN SENSE OF STYLE.

IT'S A PLACE TO COCOON, SO MAKE IT AS COMFORTABLE AS POSSIBLE.

THE ONLY PERSON YOU HAVE TO PLEASE IS YOURSELF.

### 1. BED & BREAKFAST

Sometimes a bedroom can occupy a quite unconventional position within a home. Here, the bedroom in this renovated apartment is revealed by sliding doors which open onto an unusual dining area – the centrepiece of which is a free-form concrete dining setting. The flooring stretches through the entire apartment, which is furnished in superb minimalist style. Note the cupboards going only halfway up the walls – it's a way to make the most of natural light.

### 2. ROOM TO SNOOZE

Houses in the tropics need plenty of air circulating to keep things cool. This is helped by having a central fan as well as a pitched roof. In this bedroom, the bed stands freely in the middle of the room. Storage is unobtrusive and includes drawers behind the bedhead. There's no rule to say where a bed should go – positioned in central isolation it helps create intimacy within a big space.

In these increasingly hectic times, the bedroom is a haven and a sanctuary. It is the one room in the house where you can truly get away from it all.

In most homes, it's in the bedroom where a person's true sense of style is indulged. However, bedroom design is not so much about having your possessions on show as it is about personal comfort.

Bedrooms are not always large, but beds generally are. As a consequence, the bed will usually be the focal point of the room. Choose one you really love and give a lot of thought to the way that you dress it. (See our Beds section on page 126 for some further inspiration.)

Whether you have a large or a small space, the most important thing is to make it feel comfortable and secure. Unless you like a very opulent look, it's best to try to avoid clutter in the bedroom. Think clean lines and well-chosen decorative items. A hotel-style bedroom is the newest trend, as it maximises limited space through its combination of minimalist furniture and clever storage solutions.

Customise built-in wardrobes where possible, or indulge in a walk-in wardrobe if space permits. The idea is to separate the sleeping and dressing zones. Having a computer in the bedroom is not a good idea either – work energy should be utilised elsewhere. A small desk for writing letters, however, or a comfy chair, can prove just the right addition to your bedroom.

If storage is a problem, think about getting a divan bed with built-in drawers. And don't forget blanket boxes – they are still fashionable and let you combine functionality with a decorating theme.

Include beside your bed a soft, flattering light, reading material, maybe even some flowers – whatever makes you feel happy and calm. In this room, remember, it really is all about you.

2

## 1. RELAX IN LUXURY

A warm, earthy palette can make a bedroom feel sumptuous. Situated in a high-rise apartment, this bedroom says 'luxury' rather than 'family'. It is a room to be enjoyed at night, reminiscent of a hotel bedroom. Oversized cushions and a soft-textured bedspread inspire a concept of cocooning — something of a buzzword in recent years.

## 2. INTO STORAGE

This American South-West styled bedroom has serious storage space, with a daybed built into a ceiling-height system, complete with a ladder on castors which runs the entire length of the room. Note the inspired use of contrasting prints and the overall effect of a highly personalised room; one that has been created with a distinct theme in mind.

## 3. A DREAMY SCENE

This bedroom has universal appeal. Its eclectic influences give more than a nod to the currently popular French provincial style. It is pretty without being overblown, and cosy while maintaining plenty of space. Old-world, European influences are at play here as well. If you are lucky enough to have an attractive outlook from your bedroom, as this does, make a feature of it by framing with appropriate furniture and lavish window furnishings.

## COLOURS THAT HELP YOU RELAX

**Before you begin decorating your bedroom, work out which colours make you feel good, then explore the best combinations to create a relaxing environment.**

- Blue will take the stress from your life. It's calm, restful and peaceful — but it all depends on the shade of blue. Cool blues like indigo and duck-egg blue are soothing and quiet. Sombre blues such as slate blue can make a bedroom seem oppressive and depressing.

- Purple is the colour of meditation and contemplation, and is ideal for a bedroom where you want to chill out. The lighter, warmer tones of purple — like lavender or violet — are less intrusive.

- Need nurturing? Then pink is your colour. It's physically soothing and is wonderful for lightening a mood. But go easy on the intensity — shocking pink is more confronting than comforting.

- Green brings tranquillity to a room, healing the heart and soothing emotions. Use in willowy, chartreuse or eau-de-Nil shades; avoid overly bright or sickly greens.

## DECORATIVE TRICKS FOR KIDS' ROOMS

When it comes to children's bedrooms, you need to balance their wishes with certain practicalities. For example, kids love bold colours – but today's favourite can be very quickly superseded. Try to restrict colour to the walls and to the more reasonably priced items, such as doorknobs, throws, artworks and small rugs. But always involve children in the decoration of their own room – after all it is their personal space, and the way it is kitted out should be a reflection of this.

Painted finishes you choose can add plenty of fun and zing. Murals are popular and if you are even remotely artistic you can attempt one yourself. Friezes and trompe l'oeil are also clever ways of adding colour, playfulness and originality to a child's room. Don't be afraid to go a bit wild – what child wants austerity? Instead, indulge in a scheme that brings happiness and stimulation. If your child is a budding artist, you could incorporate a large blackboard or a wall with paint that can be drawn on then wiped down clean. Big jumbo stripes, feature walls and painting partway up a wall in a different colour are all good tricks to achieve a bright, yet stylish and affordable finish. The key words should be fun and fantasy.

### 1. MURALS ADD MAGIC

Imagination can run riot in a child's bedroom – to glorious effect. Adjoining the main bedroom, this predominantly blue and white room is a kiddy wonderland, thanks to the Dr. Seuss-inspired mural. Remember, a mural can always be painted over when the child grows up, or the parents' tastes change. The raw pine cot was spray-painted white to match the overall colour scheme. Allow yourself to be creative in your child's bedroom – think back to what you may have liked, and develop your ideas from there.

### 2. OLD-WORLD WHITE

A renovated terrace home lends itself to old-world charm. This feminine yet stately bedroom draws on a French provincial theme – many of the pieces were picked up by the owners on overseas buying trips. Tucked out of the way is a modern ensuite bathroom, but the main focus is on the genteel furnishings – a Queen Anne footstool with cabriole legs, classic white linen and paint finishes, a chandelier, mantelpiece and ornate lamps. Touches of wood contrast with the room's white finishes, giving both depth and warmth.

### 3. GO GREEN

When it comes to bedrooms, the nursery is one space which shouldn't be overlooked. But how to create a nurturing yet stylish environment for a baby? This room is designed for a little boy who clearly loves planes, trains and automobiles. The furniture has been chosen with safety in mind. The soft aqua and apple-green colour scheme was inspired by the quilt cover and expanded to include the floor, curtains, walls and drawers. Basic design rules apply here, with favourite toys arranged in a group to create a stronger visual impression.

### 4. PRIMARY OPTIONS

Bold primary colours work wonderfully well in older childrens' bedrooms. Here, though, there is an extra level of sophistication, as suits two robust boys. The colour scheme takes its inspiration from the American and Australian flags (hung on the opposite wall) and the cushions and curtains were sewn to match. Storage options include funky ottoman-like boxes at the foot of each bed, and shelves bolted to the walls.

**P:** Photography
**A:** Architecture
**ID:** Interior design
**D:** Design
**S:** Styling

## FRONT COVER
**P:** Andre Martin **S:** Fiona Duff
### Pgs 2-3
**P:** Phil Aynsley
### Pg 5
**P:** Dan Magree
## CONTENTS
### Pgs 6-7
Left to right: **P:** Andre Martin
**P:** Dan Magree **P:** Andrew Lehmann
**P:** Simon Kenny **P:** Simon Kenny
## BEGINNINGS
### Pg 8
**P:** Andre Martin

## WALLS
### Pgs 10-11
1. **P:** Dan Magree **ID:** Patrick Meneguzzi, Toorak, Vic. Paintings are "Receptacle" and "Reference" by Paul Cloutier. 2. **P:** David Young **D:** Kate Platt, Kate Platt Interiors, Byron Bay, NSW.
### Pgs 12-13
1. **P:** Eric Victor-Perdraut **A&ID:** Gabriel & Elizabeth Poole Design Company, Noosaville, Qld. 2. **P:** Simon Kenny **A:** Mitch Lichtman, Campbell Luscombe Folk Lichtman, Redfern, NSW. 3. **P:** Simon Kenny **ID:** Hare + Klein, Woolloomooloo, NSW. Paintings are "Head XVII, Self Portrait '96" and "Head IX, Self Portrait '96" by John Beard.
### Pgs 14-15
1. **P:** David Morcombe **ID:** Caroline Yuen, CY Design, Shenton Park, WA. 2. **P:** Trevor Fox **D:** Mark Collingwood, Adelaide, SA. 3. **P:** Simon Kenny **ID:** Ruth Levine, RLD, Paddington, NSW. 4. **P:** Dan Magree **ID:** Patrick Meneguzzi, Toorak, Vic.
### Pgs 16-17
1. **P:** Andrew Elton **A:** Laurence Vichie, Modo Design, Canberra, ACT. 2. **P:** Dan Magree 3. **P:** David Morcombe **A:** Overman & Zuideveld, Perth, WA. 4. **P:** Andrew Elton **ID:** Bridget Tyer, Neutral Bay, NSW.

## DOORS
### Pgs 18-19
1. **P:** Dan Magree 2. **P:** Eric Victor-Perdraut **D:** Stephen Kidd, Stephen Kidd Design, Sunshine Beach, Qld.
### Pg 20-21
1. **P:** Caz Machin 2. **P:** Nigel Noyes Trompe l'oeil by Sibylla Tydeman. 3. **P:** Trevor Fox **D:** Mary Harben, Harben Design, North Adelaide, SA. 4. **P:** Jeff Kilpatrick 5. **P:** Andre Martin **ID:** Idiom, Sydney, NSW and Cox Interiors, Sydney, NSW. 6. **P:** Dan Magree **D:** Geoffrey Brown Associates, South Yarra, Vic. 7. **P:** Dan Magree **D:** Deborah Bennett, Deborah Bennett & Associates, Richmond, Vic.
### Pgs 22-23
1. **P:** Eric Victor-Perdraut **A:** Adam Smith, Push Designs, Fortitude Valley, Qld. 2. **P:** Dan Magree

## WINDOWS
### Pgs 24-25
1. **P:** Simon Kenny **ID:** Lynda Kerry Interior Design, Double Bay, NSW. 2. **P:** Dan Magree
### Pgs 26-27
1. **P:** Dan Magree 2. **P:** Andrew Elton 3. **P:** Dan Magree **ID:** Nexus Designs, South Melbourne, Vic. Painting is "Pets and their People" by Donna Brink-Reid. 4. **P:** Dan Magree **A:** Centrum Architects, South Yarra, Vic. Bronze sculpture by Peter Corlette.
### Pgs 28-29
1. **P:** Andre Martin 2. **P:** Andreas von Einsiedel **D:** Sarah Vanrenen, UK. 3. **P:** Andre Martin 4. **P:** Dan Magree
### Pgs 30-31
1. **P:** David Morcombe **ID:** Christian Lyon, Perth, WA. 2. **P:** Dan Magree 3. **P:** Dan Magree **A&D:** Michael Jan, South Melbourne, Vic. 4. **P:** Mark Green

## FLOORS
### Pg 33
1. **P:** Trevor Fox **A:** David Shannon, Shannon Architects, Prospect, SA.
### Pgs 34-35
1. **P:** Andrew Elton 2. **P:** Dan Magree **ID:** Sonia Simpfendorfer and Chelsea Hing, Nexus Designs, South Melbourne, Vic. Painting by Denise Green. 3. **P:** David Morcombe **A:** Colin Moore Architects, Subiaco, WA. 4. **P:** David Morcombe **A:** Gavin Lee, Icon Group, Cottesloe, WA. **ID:** Lisa Ciccarelli, LCD Interiors, Bicton, WA.
### Pgs 36-37
1. **P:** Simon Kenny **D:** Alexandra McKenzie Interior Design, Elizabeth Bay, NSW. Painting in centre by Joan Miró and at right by Peter Griffin. 2. **P:** Andre Martin **A:** Campbell Luscombe Folk Lichtman, Redfern, NSW. 3. **P:** Andre Martin. Artwork by Evelin.
### Pgs 38-39
1. **P:** Simon Kenny **D:** Lynda Kerry Interior Design, Double Bay, NSW. 2. **P:** Andre Martin **D:** P&S Home Furnishings, Kincumber, NSW. 3. **P:** Eric Victor-Perdraut **A:** Edge Design Group, Noosa Heads, Qld. 4. **P:** Dan Magree **A:** Iain Dykes, Kew, Vic. Painting by Michael Bowden. 5. **P:** Rodney Weidland
### Pgs 40-41
1. **P:** Andrew Elton **D:** Peter Byfield, Queens Park, NSW. 2. **P:** Andrew Elton **D:** Imagine This, Woollahra, NSW. 3. **P:** David Morcombe **A:** Craig Steere, Craig Steere, Architects, Shenton Park, WA. 4. **P:** Mark Green 5. **P:** Andrew Elton **ID:** Bridget Tyer, Neutral Bay, NSW.

## STAIRCASES
### Pgs 42-43
1. **P:** Andre Martin 2. **P:** Dan Magree **ID:** Fiona Austin, Stonehenge Group, South Melbourne, Vic.
### Pgs 44-45
1. **P:** David Morcombe **A:** Archetype Design Studio, Perth, WA. 2. **P:** Dan Magree 3. **P:** Rodney Weidland **A:** Jane Davie, Chippendale, NSW. 4. **P:** Dan Magree **A:** Centrum Architects, South Yarra, Vic. Painting by Keren Seelander. 5. **P:** Simon Kenny **A:** Tonkin Zulaikha Greer, Surry Hills, NSW.
### Pgs 46-47
1. **P:** Simon Kenny **ID:** Lambert Interiors, Rose Bay, NSW. 2. **P:** Andre Martin 3. **P:** Jeff Kilpatrick **ID:** Wall Architecture and Interiors, St Kilda, Vic.

## FIREPLACES
### Pgs 48-49
1. **P:** David Morcombe **A:** Gavin Lee, Icon Group, Cottesloe, WA. **ID:** Lisa Ciccarelli, LCD Interiors, Bicton, WA. 2. **P:** Andrew Elton **D:** Peter Byfield, Canberra, ACT. Bronze sculpture by Alex Kosmas. 3. **P:** Simon Kenny **A:** Neil Durbach, Durbach Block, Sydney, NSW.
### Pg 50
1. **P:** David Morcombe **A:** Simon Rodrigues, Odden Rodrigues Architects, Claremont, WA. Paintings by Graham Francello. 2. **P:** Andre Martin **ID:** Sharon Gallant, Gallant Design, Balmain, NSW.
### Pg 51
3. **P:** Dan Magree **A:** Neil & Idle Architects, Richmond, Vic. 4. **P:** Dan Magree **A:** Neil & Idle Architects, Richmond, Vic. Artwork in charcoal and pastel by Tim Dell. 5. **P:** Dan Magree **ID:** Patrick Meneguzzi, Toorak, Vic. 6. **P:** Eric Victor-Perdraut

## NECESSITIES
### Pg 52
**P:** Dan Magree **A&ID:** Michael Jan, Jan & Manton Design Architecture, Richmond, Vic.

## STORAGE
### Pgs 54-55
1. **P:** Dan Magree 2. **P:** Simon Kenny **ID:** Ruth Levine, RLD, Paddington, NSW.
### Pgs 56-57
1. **P:** Rodney Weidland **D:** Isabella Klompe, Paddington, NSW. 2. **P:** Dan Magree 3. **P:** Simon Kenny **ID:** Hare + Klein, Woolloomooloo, NSW. 4. **P:** Simon Kenny **ID:** Hare + Klein, Woolloomooloo, NSW. 5. **P:** Dan Magree **A:** Centrum Architects, South Yarra, Vic. Panel painted by Graham Fransella.
### Pgs 58-59
1. **P:** Dan Magree 2. **P:** Dan Magree 3. **P:** Rodney Weidland **D:** Isabella Kompe, Paddington, NSW.
### Pgs 60-61
1. **P:** Dan Magree **D:** Geoffrey Brown Associates, South Yarra, Vic. 2. **P:** Dan Magree **A:** Col Bandy, Albert Park, Vic. 3. **P:** Andre Martin **ID:** Sharon Gallant, Gallant Design, Balmain, NSW.
### Pgs 62-63
1. **P:** Trevor Fox Painting by Mark Collingwood. 2. **P:** Dan Magree 3. **P:** Dan Magree **A:** Centrum Architects, South Yarra, Vic. 4. **P:** Simon Kenny **ID:** Urban Moo, Surry Hills, NSW.

## LIGHTING
### Pgs 64-65
1. **P:** Simon Kenny 2. **P:** Dan Magree
### Pgs 66-67
1. **P:** Andre Martin **A:** Michael Folk, Campbell Luscombe Folk Lichtman, Redfern, NSW. 2. **P:** Dan Magree **ID:** Phillip Silver Interior Design, Surry Hills, NSW. 3. **P:** Eric Victor-Perdraut **A:** Paul Owen, Owen & Vokes, Fortitude Valley, Qld. 4. **P:** Mark Green **ID:** Thomas Hamel, Woollahra, NSW. Painting is "Nightfall" by Tanya Chaley.
### Pgs 68-69
1. **P:** Simon Kenny **ID:** Phillip Silver Interior Design, Surry Hills, NSW.

Photographed in the Crown Gardens Apartments. 2. **P:** David Morcombe **A:** Simon Rodrigues, Odden Rodrigues Architects, Claremont, WA. 3. **P:** Dan Magree **A:** Anthea Bickford, Toorak, Vic. 4. **P:** Andre Martin. **A:** Michael Folk, Campbell Luscombe Folk Lichtman, Redfern, NSW.
### Pgs 70-71
1. **P:** Eric Victor-Perdraut 2. **P:** Dan Magree Photographed in Lesley Kehoe Galleries, Melbourne, Vic. Vases by Kano Natsuo and 18th-century lacquer bowls. 3. **P:** Jeff Kilpatrick

## HI-TECH
### Pgs 72-73
1. **P:** Simon Kenny **A:** Mitch Lichtman, Campbell Luscombe Folk Lichtman, Redfern, NSW.
### Pgs 74-75
1. **P:** Eric Victor-Perdraut **A:** Edge Design Group, Noosa Heads, Qld. 2. **P:** Dan Magree **ID:** Fiona Austin, Stonehenge Group, South Melbourne, Vic. 3. **P:** Rodney Weidland Artwork by F Schaller. 4. **P:** Andre Martin **ID:** Meryl Hare, Hare + Klein, Woolloomooloo, NSW.
### Pgs 76-77
1. **P:** Andre Martin 2. **P:** Eric Victor-Perdraut 3. **P:** Andrew Lehmann **A:** Darryl Lock, Darryl Lock Studio, Turramurra, NSW. **ID:** Alexandra McKenzie, Alexandra McKenzie Interiors, Elizabeth Bay, NSW. 4. **P:** Simon Kenny **ID:** Alexandra McKenzie Interior Design, Elizabeth Bay, NSW.
### Pg 79
1. **P:** Andrew Elton **D:** Peter Byfield, Queens Park, NSW. 2. **P:** Simon Kenny **A:** Clark Walton, CN Walton & Associates, Glebe, NSW. Painting by Clark Walton. 3. **P:** Phil Aynsley Artwork by Gregory Pryor.

## DECORATION
### Pgs 80-81
**P:** Andrew Lehmann

## RUGS
### Pgs 82-83
1. **P:** Andre Martin **ID:** Gallant Design, Balmain, NSW. 2. **P:** Dan Magree 3. **P:** Rodney Weidland
### Pgs 84-85
1. **P:** Andre Martin **A:** Michael Folk, Campbell Luscombe Folk Lichtman, Redfern, NSW. 2. **P:** Andrew Elton 3. **P:** Rodney Weidland 4. **P:** Rodney Weidland 5. **P:** Dan Magree Painting by Maureen O'Shaunessy.
### Pgs 86-87
1. **P:** Trevor Fox **A:** Richard Stafford, Adelaide, SA. 2. **P:** Ben Rollison **S:** Fiona Duff

## CARPETS
### Pgs 88-89
1. **P:** Andrew Elton **ID:** Bridget Tyer, Neutral Bay, NSW. 2. **P:** Simon Kenny **ID:** Lynda Kerry Interior Design, Double Bay, NSW.
### Pgs 90-91
1. **P:** Simon Kenny **ID:** Hare + Klein, Woolloomooloo, NSW. 2. **P:** Simon Kenny **A:** David Yee, Zetland, NSW. 3. **P:** David Morcombe **A&ID:** Neil

Cownie, Overman & Zuideveld, Northbridge, WA. **4. P:** Dean Wilmot **ID:** Thomas Bucich, Thomas Bucich Design, Paddington, NSW. **5. P:** Dan Magree **ID:** Jenny Goble, Pomp, St Kilda, Vic.

**Pgs 92-93**
**1. P:** Dan Magree **2. P:** Dan Magree **ID:** Jenny Goble, Pomp, St Kilda, Vic. **3. P:** Dan Magree

ART

**Pgs 94-95**
**1. P:** Dan Magree Painting by Sean Parker. **2. P:** Andrew Elton Paintings by Marie Hegarty.

**Pgs 96-97**
**1. P:** Andreas von Einsiedel **2. P:** Andrew Elton Paintings by Alex Kosmas. **3. P:** Dan Magree **ID:** Jennie Goble, Pomp, St Kilda, Vic. Painting by Gavin Brown.

**Pgs 98-99**
**1. P:** Dan Magree **2. P:** Ben Rollison **3. P:** Trevor Fox Paintings by Nella de Pizzol. **4. P:** Trevor Fox

ACCESSORIES

**Pgs 100-101**
**1. P:** Simon Kenny **2. P:** Simon Kenny **ID:** Lambert Interiors, Rose Bay, NSW.

**Pgs 102-103**
**1. P:** Dan Magree Painting by Terri Frasier. **2. P:** Dan Magree **3. P:** Dan Magree

**Pgs 104-105**
**1. P:** Dan Magree **ID:** Fiona Austin, Stonehenge Group, South Melbourne, Vic. **2. P:** Dan Magree **3. P:** Dan Magree **D:** Hermon & Hermon, Richmond, Vic. **4. P:** Nigel Noyes Handcrafted pottery by Giuseppe Matteo Pappalardo. **5. P:** Dan Magree Paintings by Helen Guek Wee Mei.

**Pgs 106-107**
**1. P:** Simon Griffiths **2. P:** Andrew Lehmann **3. P:** Rob Reichenfeld

COMFORT

**Pgs 108-109**
**P:** Simon Kenny **S:** Prue Trollope, Rozelle, NSW.

SEATING

**Pgs 110-111**
**1. P:** Simon Kenny **ID:** Ruth Levine, RLD, Paddington, NSW. Painting by Richard Allen. **2. P:** David Morcombe Painting by Waldemar Kolbusz.

**Pgs 112-113**
**1. P:** Simon Kenny **ID:** Alexandra McKenzie Interiors, Sydney, NSW. **2. P:** Phil Aynsley **A:** Philip Corben, Corben Architects, Neutral Bay, NSW. **3. P:** Trevor Fox **A:** Con Bastiras, Kings Park, SA. **4. P:** David Morcombe **A:** Gorki Bogdanich and Lynette Chew-Bogdanich, Archetype Design Studio, Perth, WA. **5. P:** Andre Martin

**Pgs 114-115**
**1. P:** Eric Victor-Perdraut **2. P:** Dan Magree **A:** Iain Dykes, Kew, Vic. **3. P:** Andre Martin **ID:** Sharon Gallant, Gallant Design, Balmain, NSW. **4. P:** Simon Kenny **ID:** Phillip Silver Interior Design, Surry Hills, NSW. **5. P:** Dan Magree

**Pgs 116-117**
**1. P:** Simon Kenny **ID:** Ruth Levine, RLD, Paddington, NSW. **2. P:** Dan Magree **A:** Michael Jan, Jan & Manton Design

Architecture, Richmond, Vic. Painting by Tim McGuire. **3. P:** Simon Griffiths Painting by John Wallen. **4. P:** Andrew Elton Paintings by Marie Hagerty. Sculpture by Peter Vandermark.

**Pgs 118-119**
**1. P:** Eric Victor-Perdraut **2. P:** Dan Magree **3. P:** Dan Magree **ID:** Elise Fayers, Candlewick Interior Design and Decoration, Hawthorn, Vic. **4. P:** Caz Machin

TABLES

**Pgs 120-121**
**1. P:** Dan Magree Painting by Graham Fransella from Axia Modern Art. **2. P:** Andrew Lehmann **ID:** Alexandra McKenzie Interiors, Elizabeth Bay, NSW.

**Pgs 122-123**
**1. P:** Ben Rollison **S:** Fiona Duff **2. P:** Phil Aynsley **S:** Fiona Duff **3. P:** Maree Homer **4. P:** Eric Victor-Perdraut **D:** Adam Smith, Push Design, Fortitude Valley, Qld.

**Pgs 124-125**
**1. P:** David Morcombe **A:** Colin Moore, Subiaco, WA. Artworks by David Watts. **2. P:** Andre Martin **3. P:** Dan Magree **4. P:** Simon Kenny **ID:** Lynda Kerry, Lynda Kerry Interior Design, Double Bay, NSW.

BEDS

**Pgs 126-127**
**1. P:** David Morcombe **2. P:** Simon Kenny **ID:** Leroy Belle, Darlinghurst, NSW.

**Pgs 128-129**
**1. P:** Andrew Elton **2. P:** Maree Homer **3. P:** Phil Aynsley **4. P:** Dan Magree **5. P:** Simon Griffiths **6. P:** Andrew Elton

ECLECTIC

**Pgs 130-131**
**1. P:** Andrew Elton **2. P:** Rodney Weidland

**Pgs 132-133**
**1. P:** Andrew Lehmann **2. P:** Dan Magree Paintings by Helen Guek Wee Mei. **3. P:** Simon Kenny **A:** David Yee, Zetland, NSW. **4. P:** Ray Clarke

**Pgs 134-135**
**1. P:** Dan Magree **2. P:** Dan Magree **3. P:** Simon Kenny **ID:** Leroy Belle, Darlinghurst, NSW. **4. P:** Dan Magree

**Pgs 136-137**
**1. P:** Jeff Kilpatrick **2. P:** Simon Kenny **3. P:** Nigel Noyes Fabric design by Deborah Leser, Sydney, NSW.

LIVING

**Pgs 138-139**
**P:** Simon Kenny **ID:** Leroy Belle, Darlinghurst, NSW.

LIVING SPACES

**Pgs 140-141**
**1. P:** Dan Magree **S:** Emma Star Hamwood **2. P:** Eric Victor-Perdraut **A&ID:** Gabriel & Elizabeth Poole Design Company, Noosaville, Qld.

**Pgs 142-143**
**1. P:** Simon Kenny Painting in the dining area is "Untitled", a self portrait by John Beard. **2. P:** Dan Magree **ID:** Geoffrey Brown, South Yarra, Vic. **3. P:** Andrew Elton **ID:** Susie McIntosh, Fleur De Levande, Sydney, NSW. **4. P:** Andre Martin **A:** Michael Folk, Campbell Luscombe Folk Lichtman, Redfern, NSW.

**Pgs 144-145**
**1. P:** Jeff Kilpatrick **2. P:** Andrew Elton **3. P:** Mark Green **ID:** Thomas Hamel, Woollahra, NSW. **4. P:** Dan Magree **A:** Leon Meyer, Inform Design and Construction, Sandringham, Vic. **5. P:** Dan Magree **D:** Hermon & Hermon, Richmond, Vic.

**Pgs 146-147**
**1. P:** Ben Rollison **S:** Fiona Duff **2. P:** Dan Magree **ID:** Robyn Nedovic, Toorak, Vic. Painting is "Peaceful Landscape" by Melissa Egan. **3. P:** Rodney Weidland

**Pgs 148-149**
**1. P:** Simon Kenny **ID:** Phillip Silver Interior Design, Surry Hills, NSW. **2. P:** Simon Kenny **ID:** Lynda Kerry Interior Design, Double Bay, NSW. **3. P:** Bill Anagrius

TRANSITIONS

**Pg 151**
**1. P:** Dan Magree **A:** Anthea Bickford, Toorak, Vic.

**Pg 152-153**
**1. P:** Simon Kenny **ID:** Phillip Silver Interior Design, Surry Hills, NSW. **2. P:** David Morcombe **A:** Odden Rodrigues Architect, Claremont, WA. **3. P:** Andre Martin **ID:** Hare + Klein, Woolloomooloo, NSW.

**Pg 155**
**1. P:** Simon Kenny **A&ID:** Urban Moo, Surry Hills, NSW. **2. P:** David Morcombe **D:** Wal Kolbusz, North Perth, WA. **3. P:** Andrew Lehmann **A:** Valerie Martin **A:** Caroline Pidcock, Surry Hills, NSW.

KITCHENS + LAUNDRIES

**Pgs 156-157**
**1. P:** Andrew Lehmann **ID:** Paulette Mirzikinian, Basicz, Sydney, NSW. **2. P:** Eric Victor-Perdraut **D:** Carole Tretheway and Stephen Kidd, Kidd + Co Designers, Sunshine Beach, Qld.

**Pgs 158-159**
**1. P:** Simon Kenny **A:** Mitch Lichtman, Campbell Luscombe Folk Lichtman, Redfern, NSW. **2. P:** Andrew Elton **ID:** Imagine This, Woollahra, NSW. **3. P:** Dan Magree **ID:** Susie McIntosh, Fleur De Levande, Melbourne, Vic.

**Pgs 160-161**
**1. P:** David Morcombe **ID:** Paul Cox, Barber Interior Design, West Leederville, WA. **2. P:** Jack Sarafian **A:** Frank Lordanic, Barwon Heads, Vic. Painting by Monica Adams. **3. P:** Dan Magree

**Pgs 162-163**
**1. P:** Eric Victor-Perdraut **D:** Kitchens by Kathie, Brisbane, Qld. **2. P:** David Morcombe **D:** Wal Kolbusz, North Perth, WA. **3. P:** Alan Benson **D:** D'Abblers, Canberra, ACT.

**Pgs 164-165**
**1. P:** Eric Victor-Perdraut **2. P:** Dan Magree **A:** David Neil Architects, Canterbury, Vic. **3. P:** David Morcombe **ID:** Marco Iannantuoni, Jolimont, WA. **A:** John Collier, CMP, Perth, WA. **4. P:** David Morcombe **A:** Colin Moore, Subiaco, WA.

BATHROOMS

**Pgs 166-167**
**1. P:** Andrew Elton **2. P:** Sharyn Cairns **A:** Russell Casper, Grodski Architects, Prahran, Vic.

**Pgs 168-169**
**1. P:** Andrew Elton **D:** Robyn Kennedy, Imagine This, Woollahra, NSW. **2. P:** Simon Kenny **A:** Alex Coutts & Associates, Northbridge, NSW. **3. P:** Andre Martin **4. P:** Andrew Elton **D:** M-Design Tiles & Bathrooms, Fyshwick, ACT.

**Pgs 170-171**
**1. P:** Trevor Fox **ID:** Con Bastiras, Kings Park, SA. **2. P:** David Morcombe **ID:** Paul Cox, Barber Interior Design, West Leederville, WA. **3. P:** Ray Clarke **D:** Jilly Hampshire, Double Bay, NSW. **4. P:** Rodney Weidland **A:** Caroline Pidcock, Darlinghurst, NSW. **5. P:** Simon Kenny **ID:** Phillip Silver Interior Design, Surry Hills, NSW. **6. P:** Martin Saunders **ID:** Olsen ID, Armadale, Vic.

DAY SPAS

**Pgs 172-173**
**1. P:** Ben Rollison **2. P:** Dan Magree **D:** Peter Stepic, Melbourne, Vic.

**Pgs 174-175**
Thanks to Fitness Inside Out, Darlinghurst, NSW, for the "Home gym essentials" information.
**1. P:** David Morcombe **ID:** Marco Iannantuoni, Jolimont, WA. **2. P:** Eric Victor Perdraut **3. P:** Eric Victor Perdraut **4. P:** Simon Kenny **ID:** Ruth Levine, RLD, Paddington, NSW. **5. P:** Trevor Fox

HOME OFFICES

**Pgs 176-177**
**1&2. P:** Simon Kenny **A:** Duncan Reed, Utz Sanby Architects, Crows Nest, NSW.

**Pgs 178-179**
**1. P:** Dan Magree Photographed at Lesley Kehoe Galleries, Melbourne, Vic. **2. P:** Bill Anagrius **ID:** Babette Hayes Designs, Mosman, NSW. **3. P:** Simon Kenny Cupboard by Woodhill Classics, Berry, NSW. **4. P:** Jeff Kilpatrick **ID:** Babette Hayes Designs, Mosman, NSW. **5. P:** Phil Aynsley

**Pgs 180-181**
**1. P:** Andreas von Einsiedel **A:** Peter Wadley, UK. **2. P:** David Morcombe **A:** Hofman & Brown Architects, Cottesloe, WA. **3. P:** David Morcombe **4. P:** Bill Anagrius

BEDROOMS

**Pgs 182-183**
**1. P:** Simon Kenny **2. P:** Eric Victor-Perdraut

**Pgs 184-185**
**1. P:** Simon Kenny **2. P:** Richard Powers **3. P:** Dan Magree

**Pgs 186-187**
**1. P:** Andrew Elton **2. P:** Andrew Elton **3. P:** John Best **4. P:** Simon Kenny

AUSTRALIAN HOUSE & GARDEN: DECOR
**Editor-in-chief** Anny Friis
**Editor** Rose-Marie Hillier
**Text** Rose-Marie Hillier, Julie Simpkin, Rowena Mary, Jo McKinnon

ACP BOOKS
**Creative director** Hieu Chi Nguyen
**Designer** Alison Windmill
**Copy editor** Jo McKinnon
**Publishing manager (sales)** Brian Cearnes
**Publishing manager (rights & new projects)** Jane Hazell
**Marketing manager** Sarah Cave
**Production manager** Carol Currie
**Business manager** Seymour Cohen
**Assistant business analyst** Martin Howes
**Studio manager** Caryl Wiggins
**Pre-press** Harry Palmer
**Editorial coordinator** Caroline Lowry
**Editorial assistant** Karen Lai
**Group publisher** Pat Ingram
**Publisher** Sue Wannan
**Editorial director** Susan Tomnay
**Chief executive officer** John Alexander

Produced by **ACP**books
Printed by SNP Leefung, China
Published by ACP Publishing Pty Limited,
54 Park St, Sydney; GPO Box 4088,
Sydney, NSW 2001.
Ph: (02) 9282 8618  Fax: (02) 9267 9438.
acpbooks@acp.com.au
www.acpbooks.com.au
AUSTRALIA: Distributed by Network Services, GPO Box 4088, Sydney, NSW 2001.
Ph: (02) 9282 8777  Fax: (02) 9264 3278.
UNITED KINGDOM: Distributed by Australian Consolidated Press (UK), Moulton Park Business
Centre, Red House Road,
Moulton Park, Northampton, NN3 6AQ.
Ph: (01604) 497531  Fax: (01604) 497533  acpukltd@aol.com
CANADA: Distributed by Whitecap Books Ltd,
351 Lynn Avenue, North Vancouver, BC, V7J 2C4.
Ph: (604) 980 9852  Fax: (604) 980 8197
customerservice@whitecap.ca
www.whitecap.ca
NEW ZEALAND: Distributed by Netlink Distribution Company, ACP Media Centre,
Cnr Fanshawe and Beaumont streets, Westhaven, Auckland.
PO Box 47906, Ponsonby, Auckland, NZ.
Ph: (09) 366 9966  ask@ndcnz.co.nz

Australian House & Garden: Decor.
Includes index.
ISBN 1 86396 371 5.
1. Interior decoration  Australia. 2. House furnishings  Australia. I. Title.
747.0994

Front cover: Photography by Andre Martin.  Styling by Fiona Duff.

# FISH & SEAFOOD

# **Colo**phon

© 2003 Rebo International b.v., Lisse, The Netherlands

www.rebo-publishers.com - info@rebo-publishers.com

Original recipes and photographs: © R&R Publishing Pty. Ltd.

Design, layout and typesetting: R&R Publishing Pty. Ltd., Victoria, Australia

Cover design: Minkowsky Graphics, Enkhuizen, The Netherlands

Proofreading: Jarmila Pešková Škraňáková, Joshua H. Joseph

ISBN 90 366 1609 3

# FISH & SEAFOOD

the best from the seven seas for

## creative cooking

REBO
PUBLISHERS

# **Fore**word

All waterways offer flavors to complement every occasion, from a casual barbecue to a formal dinner, and everything in between. In addition to offering a wealth of flavors, seafood is affordable, easy to prepare, and offers a wide range of health benefits to those who eat it.

Seafood is an integral part of any lifestyle. Whether it is a hot summer's day, or in the middle of winter, we will choose a seafood dish to complement the occasion. That is one of the beauties of Fresh Food Cooking with Seafood. It offers traditional European recipes, as well as Asian and modern Australian dishes. *Fish and seafood* breaks down many of the perceived barriers people have about cooking with seafood. Simple step-by-step pictures show the ease with which any type of seafood can be prepared for cooking. Because these recipes incorporate seafood, they are not only tasty, but healthy as well.

We are increasingly conscious of the importance of sensible eating habits, and seafood is an important element to include in a well-balanced diet. Seafood contains, on average, less than 2 percent fat. This is lower than most chicken cuts and much lower than lean red meat. Seafood is particularly good for those on low-fat diets.

Research shows that eating fish two or three times a week can help lower cholesterol and reduce the risk of heart disease. Seafood is an excellent source of top quality protein and minerals, including iodine, zinc, potassium and phosphorus. It is also rich in vitamins, especially the B group. The small amount of fat in fish is rich in Omega-3 fatty acids, making fish a great heart food. Omega-3 fatty acids from fish can prevent blood clots from forming, thus reducing the risk of heart attack.

Recent studies show that eating seafood reduced joint stiffness and pain from rheumatoid arthritis, and that consumption of fresh, oily fish is associated with a significantly reduced risk of asthma in children.

# **Meas**urements

All measurements conform to European
and American measurement systems.
For easier cooking, the American cup
measurement is used throughout the book.

tbsp = tablespoon
tsp = teaspoon
oz = ounce
lb = pound
°F = degrees Fahrenheit
°C = degrees Celsius
g = gram
kg = kilogram
cm = centimeter
ml = mililiter
l = liter

**Rinse** salmon under cold running water, pat dry, and set aside. In shallow glass dish, combine all but last two ingredients. Place salmon in marinade. Cover, and refrigerate for 1-2 hours.

**Remove** from refrigerator and bring to room temperature. Remove salmon from marinade and reserve the liquid. Cook salmon, pepper, and onion on well-oiled barbecue (or grill over medium heat) for 6-7 minutes (or until lightly browned). Brush with marinade, turn.

**Brush** again. Continue cooking for another 5 minutes (or until flesh is opaque when fork-tested). To serve: top fillets with grilled pepper and onion.

## Ingredients

4 x Atlantic Salmon fillets

1 cup dry red wine

½ cup olive oil

½ cup lemon juice

2 shallots (chopped)

2 tsp freshly crushed garlic

1 tsp freshly crushed ginger

1 tsp salt

½ tsp rosemary leaves

¼ tsp Tabasco

4 large pepper rings

4 large slices white onion

**Grilled** Salmon Fillets

**Preheat** oven to 360°F/ 180°C. Heat olive oil in a saucepan. Add onion and garlic, and cook (until onion is transparent). Add tarragon and tomato paste, and stir for 3-4 minutes. Add tarragon and tomato paste, and stir for 3-4 minutes.

**Add** wine, tomatoes, anchovies and olives, and cook until tomatoes are soft up. Cut 4 pieces of aluminium foil into 12in/30cm-squares. Place foil shiny side-down, and put fillet in the centre. Spoon sauce mixture on top of fillet.

**Spoon** sauce mixture on top of fillet. Bring opposite sides of foil together, the fold down twice and fold ends to close. Place in preheated oven at 356°F/ 180°C for approximately 25 minutes.

## Ingredients

4 barramundi fillets (approximately 7oz/200g each)

**Sauce**

4 tsp olive oil

1 large onion (finely diced)

2 tsp freshly crushed garlic

½ cup white wine

2 tsp tarragon leaves

1 tbsp tomato paste

8 medium tomatoes peeled and diced

4 anchovy fillets (chopped fine)

4½ oz/125g pitted olives

## **Barramundi** Putanesca

**To make** chive oil, mix all ingredients together, and set aside (for at least 4 hours). Ideally make the chive oil a day before use.

**To make polenta:** heat butter and onion for 2-3 minutes in a medium-sized saucepan until transparent, pour in milk, and bring to boil. Whisk in the polenta and continue to whisk until thickened. Season to taste with salt and pepper.

**Season** fish, and brush with olive oil. Chargrill until just cooked. Serve by spooning soft polenta on a serving plate, add fish and drizzle chive oil over the top. Place baby rocket leaves around fish.

# **Chargrilled** Blackfish with Chive Oil and Polenta

## Ingredients

1lb 4oz/1kg blackfish or luderick fillets

baby rocket leaves (for serving)

### Chive oil

½ cup extra virgin oil

2 bunches fresh chives (chopped)

pinch rock salt

pinch black peppercorns (freshly ground)

### Polenta

3 tbsp butter

1 small onion (finely chopped)

3⅓ cups milk

½ cup polenta

black peppercorns (freshly ground)

salt

**Preheat** oven to moderate temperature (350°F/ 180°C). Mix onion, parsley, and celery leaves together, and sprinkle onto base of a large, greased, shallow baking dish.

**Sprinkle** the curry powder, pepper, and salt on both sides of cutlets. Arrange cutlets on parsley mixture, and place half a slice of bacon on each. Bake uncovered in a moderately hot oven for 25-30 minutes (or until fish flakes easily when gently pierced).

**Lift** fish onto warm serving plates. Serve topped with slices of Maître d'Hôtel butter and a crisp salad. To make Maître d'Hôtel butter, blend all ingredients together. Form into a log shape on a piece of plastic wrap and roll up. Chill until firm.

# **Baked** Cod Cutlets with Maître d'Hôtel Butter

### Ingredients

1 medium onion (finely chopped)

1 cup fresh parsley sprigs

1 cup celery leaves (roughly chopped)

6 blue eye cutlets

1½ tsp madras curry powder

salt and pepper (to taste)

3 slices bacon

### Maître d'hôtel Butter

4½ oz/125g softened butter

2 tbsp lemon juice

2 tsp finely chopped parsley

salt and freshly ground black pepper (to taste)

13

**Preheat** oven to moderate (365°F/180°C). Thinly slice cucumber and mushrooms, and layer half into a greased casserole dish. Put fish on top, and season with salt and pepper. Sprinkle combined lemon juice and chili sauce over fish, and top with remaining cucumber and mushrooms.

**Pour** wine over fish, and dot with 3 tbsp butter. Cover and cook in a moderate oven for 30 minutes or until fish is tender. Remove fish with cucumber and mushrooms to heated plates and keep warm.

**Drain** liquid from pan into a small saucepan, bring to boil, and boil rapidly adding remaining butter in small pieces. When liquid is reduced to a light glaze, pour over fish.

# **Bream** with Cucumber

## **Ingredients**

2 small cucumbers

4½ oz/125g button mushrooms

4 whole bream

1 tbsp lemon juice

1 tbsp sweet chili sauce

½ cup dry white wine

6 tbsp butter

salt and pepper

**Sprinkle** fish with salt. Cut a 2 in/5cm piece from each spring onion at the bulb-end, and cut the green parts lengthwise into strips, set them aside. Place the spring onion bulbs into a heat-proof dish 1in/ 2.5cm smaller than the steamer to be used. Place fish in the dish, and top with ginger slices.

**Combine** the soy sauce, sherry, sugar, and stock. Spoon it over the fish and marinate for 20 minutes basting once or twice. When ready to cook, place fish in a fish steamer lined with foil.

**Cover** tightly, and steam over high heat for 15-20 minutes until the fish is just barely opaque through the thickest point. With a knife, pierce the fish along the back at the thickest part, and gently lift the blade to check for doneness.

**Just** before serving, heat the oil and garlic in a small pan until very hot. When garlic begins to color, remove and discard it keeping the oil. Remove the plate of fish from the steamer. Scatter the coriander and the tangle of reserved green onion strips on the surface, and pour the hot oil over all. Serve immediately.

### Ingredients

750g coral trout (cleaned and gutted)

½ tsp salt

4 spring onions (trimmed)

4 slices ginger (unpeeled)

2 tbsp soy sauce

2 tbsp dry sherry

½ tsp sugar

⅓ cup basic fish stock (page 39)

2 tbsp oil

1 clove garlic (split lengthwise)

2½oz/65g coriander leaves

**Steamed** Coral Trout with Ginger, Green Onions, and Coriander

**In** a large saucepan, heat the oil and sauté the celery and onion. Add tomatoes, garlic, herbs, and Worcestershire sauce. Mix in the chicken stock. Simmer for 1 hour.

**Add** potato. Taste and adjust seasoning if necessary. Add wine and tomato juice, then simmer for another 2 hours.

**Add** the cod and jewfish first, after a minute add the mussels and scallops. Simmer 1 minute then add the shrimp and crayfish cubes.

# **Delicious** Bouillabaisse

### Ingredients

2 tbsp olive oil

½ bunch celery tops (chopped)

2 large onions (chopped)

2 x 1lb 12oz/750g cans chopped tomatoes

2 tsp crushed garlic

1 tbsp chopped basil

1 tbsp chopped parsley

1 tsp dried thyme

2 tbsp Worcestershire sauce

1½ cups chicken stock

1 large potato (chopped)

1½ cups dry white wine

2 cups tomato juice

12 mussels (scrubbed)

15 medium shrimp (deveined and shelled)

8 scallops (shucked)

1 crayfish tail, flesh removed and diced

4½ oz/125g can crabmeat (or fresh if available)

9oz/250g jewfish or perch, cubed

9oz/250g blue eye cod, cubed

crusty bread for serving

**Melt** butter in a sauce-pan, add onion, cumin and coriander and cook while stirring for 1 minute. Add remaining ingredients and stir over moderate heat for about 5 minutes until sauce thickens. Set aside and cover to keep warm.

**Sprinkle** lemon juice over fillets and brush with melted butter.

**Grill** under a hot grill or on a greased grill or grid-dle plate for 2-3 minutes each side or until cooked through. Remove to a heated plate, top with a spoonful of tahini peanut sauce and garnish with fresh coriander leaves and lemon wedges. Serve immediately.

# **Silver** Dory with Tahini–Peanut Sauce

**Ingredients**

1lb/500g silver dory fillets

2 tbsp lemon juice

3 tbsp butter, melted

**Tahini and sesame sauce**

3 tbsp butter

1 tsp ground cumin seeds

1 tsp finely chopped fresh coriander leaves

1 medium onion finely chopped

2 tbsp sweet sherry

2 tbsp tahini

2 tbsp peanut butter

1 tbsp honey

1 tbsp lemon juice

¼ cup water

**Make** the cucumber dressing, mix all ingredients together in a bowl. Cover the bowl with plastic wrap and refrigerate well before use.

**Combine** the breadcrumbs lemon rind, curry powder, parsley, and tumeric. Coat the fish with flour, shaking off excess. Dip into beaten eggs then cover with bread-crumbs. Pressing crumbs on firmly. Refrigerate for 30 minutes.

**Heat** oil ¼in/½cm deep in frying pan, add fish and cook 3 minutes each side or until cooked through. Drain on absorbent paper. Serve immediately with cucumber sauce.

## Ingredients

4oz/120g fresh breadcrumbs

3 tsp lemon rind (grated)

2 tsp madras

curry powder

1 tbsp parsley flakes

1 tbsp dill leaf tips

1 tsp ground turmeric

8 flathead fillets

plain flour

2 eggs (lightly beaten)

oil (for shallow frying)

### Cucumber Dressing

8 fl oz/250ml yogurt

2 tbsp fresh chopped mint

1 small cucumber (finely diced)

1 tsp freshly crushed garlic

1 tsp caster sugar

**Lemon** Crusted Flathead

**To make sauce:** combine milk, parsley, bayleaf, peppercorns and onion in a saucepan, and heat. Remove and strain the milk. Melt butter in saucepan, add flour, and cook, stirring (over low heat), for 2 minutes. Remove from heat and gradually add warm milk mixture.

**Return** to moderate heat and cook stirring constantly until mixture boils and thickens. Add cream and shelled shrimp.

**Sprinkle** fillets with lemon juice, and lightly coat with seasoned flour. Melt butter in frying pan, add fish, and cook (until golden brown and tender). Remove to a serving dish. Gently reheat the sauce over the fish and spoon. Serve immediately.

## Ingredients

1lb/500g flounder fillets

lemon juice

seasoned flour

4½oz/125g butter

**Sauce**

1½ cups milk

¼ tsp parsley flakes

1 bay leaf

6 black peppercorns

1 tbsp onion (finely chopped)

4 tbsp butter

3 tbsp plain flour

½ cup cream

150g cooked shrimp

**Flounder** with Shrimp Sauce

**To make sweet chilli sauce:** deseed and finely chop the chili. Chop the coriander roots and garlic. Mix the sugar, vinegar, and water together in a saucepan and bring to a boil. Remove from heat and add the chopped chili, coriander root and leaves, garlic, and fish sauce. Cover and stand aside to cool.

**Mix** the Szechuan pepper, cornflour, and five-spice powder together and lightly coat the garfish fillets.

**Heat**, oil for deep frying to 350°F/180°C. Add the coated fish fillets and cook for 2 minutes until golden color and cooked through. Serve with a mixed green salad and the sweet chili sauce in a small dish on the side for dipping.

# **Chinese** Garfish Fillets

## Ingredients

½ tsp Szechwan ground pepper

3 tbsp cornflour

1½ tsp Chinese five-spice powder

1 tsp salt

2lb 4oz/1kg garfish fillets (all bones removed; skin on)

oil for deep frying

mixed green salad to serve

## Sweet Chili Sauce

3 large red chilies

2 cloves garlic, finely chopped

3 tbsp chopped coriander leaves

4 coriander roots

9oz/250g sugar

⅔ cup Thai coconut vinegar

⅔ cup water

2 tbsp Thai fish sauce

**Preheat** oven to 375°F/190°C. Boil the potatoes then mash with butter and hot milk. Spread on base of a large greased ovenproof dish.

**Spread** one-third of the sour cream over the potatoes and sprinkle with chopped onion.

**Arrange** fish over the top and sprinkle with combined bread-crumbs and cheese. Spread remaining sour cream over crumbs and sprinkle with paprika. Bake in preheated oven for 30-35 minutes until fish is cooked brown and top browned. To serve, cut into squares. Top each serving with a spoonful of remaining sour cream and sprinkle with paprika.

# **Gemfish** Potato Casserole

## **Ingredients**

6 medium potatoes

3 tbsp butter

⅓ cup hot milk

1¼ cups sour cream

1 small onion (finely chopped)

6 gemfish fillets

⅓ cup dry breadcrumbs

2 tbsp cheese (grated)

ground paprika

**Preheat** oven to moderate temperature (350°F/ 180°C). Arrange fish in a shallow ovenproof dish which has been lightly brushed with olive oil. Brush the top of each cutlet with olive oil.

**Combine** parsley, garlic, almonds, shallots, paprika, lemon rind, and 1½ tablespoons olive oil. Spoon over fish, and press down well.

**Bake** fish in a moderate oven for 10 minutes. Pour the tomatoes around the fish, and cook for a further 10 minutes or until fish is cooked.

# **Spanish** Style Fish Cutlets

## Ingredients

4 jewfish cutlets

olive oil

1 tbsp finely chopped parsley

3 tsp freshly crushed garlic

1oz/30g almonds (slivered)

1 tbsp green onions (chopped)

½ tsp ground paprika

½ tsp lemon rind (grated)

15oz/425g can tomatoes

(drained and roughly chopped)

**Mix** butter and mustard in a small bowl until smooth. Add capers, salt, and pepper, then mix well. Spread equal amounts evenly over each fillet. Sprinkle paprika on top.

**Place** fillets in a large micro-wave safe dish and cover with plastic wrap folding back one edge to allow steam to escape.

**Cook** on high until opaque throughout (about 5-7 minutes, depending on thickness of fillets). Let stand for at least 2 minutes (covered) before serving. Serve with a selection of steamed vegetables.

# **Kingfish** with Mustard and Capers

### Ingredients

4 tbsp butter (softened)

1 tbsp Dijon mustard

1 tbsp capers (chopped)

½ tsp salt

½ tsp cracked black peppercorns

4 x kingfish cutlets (each 6–9oz/185–250g)

¼ tsp ground paprika

**Preheat** oven to moderate temperature (356°F/180°C). Place each cutlet on a piece of greased, heavy-duty aluminium foil. Season with pepper and lemon juice.

**Divide** grated cheese among cutlets. Sprinkle with spring onions, and top each cutlet with cucumber slices (about 4–6 slices on each cutlet).

**Fold** down the foil, double fold and seal ends. Place on oven tray and bake in a preheated, moderately hot oven (for 20–25 minutes).

# **Fish** in a Parcel

## **Ingredients**

4 mackerel cutlets

freshly ground black peppercorns

1 tbsp lemon juice

2¼ oz/65g tasty cheese (grated)

4 spring onions or green onion (chopped)

1 medium cucumber (sliced)

35

**Preheat** oven to 430°F/ 220°C. Place each fillet in center of a piece of heavy duty aluminium foil. Drizzle 1 tbsp of oil over each.

**Crumble** equal amount of feta cheese over each fillet and scatter olives on top.

**Sprinkle** each fillet with a little lemon juice and season with salt and pepper. Fold the foil over with a double fold and seal the ends. Place packets on a baking tray. Bake 10-12 minutes in preheated hot oven. Stand 10 minutes before opening packages. Serve with salad garnish.

# **Greek** Style Mullet with Olives and Feta

### Ingredients

4 x mullet fillets

4 tbsp olive oil

4½ oz/125g feta cheese

9oz/250g black olives (pitted, coarsely chopped)

2 tsp fresh lemon juice

½ tsp cracked black peppercorns

**Combine** the water, lemon juice, stock cubes, shallots, thyme, and pepper in a deep frypan. Bring liquid to boil. Cover, and simmer for 5 minutes. Add carrot, and let simmer for an extra 4 minutes.

**Lay** the fillets in the liquid without crowding. Cover, and simmer for about 10 minutes (until fish is opaque and flakes easily).

**Remove** fish and keep hot. Boil remaining liquid in pan until it reduces and thickens slightly. Serve the fish on a bed of prepared wild rice and spoon over the liquid and vegetables from the pan.

# **Poached** Orange Roughy on Wild Rice

## Ingredients

1 cup water

2 tbsp lemon juice

2 sqeeze-on chicken stocks

4½ oz/125g spring onions (sliced diagonally)

¼ tsp thyme leaves

¼ tsp ground white pepper

4½ oz/125g carrots (thinly sliced diagonally)

1lb 2oz/500g orange roughy fillets

9oz/250g wild rice (prepared according to packet directions)

round paprika (for garnish)

fish & seafood

39

**Preheat** oven to 350°F/ 180°C. Cut vegetables into 4in/10cm thin strips. Place fillets and season with pepper and salt. Divide vegetable strips amongst fillets, and roll up around vegetables. Secure with toothpicks.

**Place** fish rolls in baking dish, spoon lemon juice over, cover, and bake in a moderately hot oven for 20 minutes (or until cooked through). To make the sauce, melt butter in a saucepan, add onions and garlic, and cook, stirring (until onions are soft).

**Add** wine, tomatoes, tomato paste, and salt and pepper to taste. Bring to a boil, reduce heat, and simmer (until sauce is slightly thickened). Add basil, and stir well. Spoon sauce over fish rolls.

# **Perch** Rolls with Tomato Basil Sauce

### Ingredients

1 zucchini

1 carrot

1 stick celery

4 perch fillets

salt and pepper

1 tbsp lemon juice

### Sauce

2 tbsp butter

1 medium onion (finely chopped)

1 tsp freshly crushed garlic

½ cup dry white wine

4 large tomatoes (peeled, seeded, and chopped)

1 tbsp tomato paste

salt and pepper

1 tbsp chopped fresh basil leaves

**To make marinated peppers:** roast peppes skin-side up until chared, about 5 minutes. Place in a plastic bag and close. When cool, peel off the skin. Place into a non-metallic dish, mix the olive oil, basil, oregano, garlic, salt and pepper together. Pour over the pepper strips, cover, and stand 20 minutes or more to marinate.

**Preheat** oven to 390°F/ 200°C. Brush tomato halves with the oil and sprinkle with the white breadcrumbs. Place on an oiled shallow baking tray.

**Place** the fillets onto a large oiled baking dish; season with salt and pepper and sprinkle over the wine. Place tomatoes and fish in the preheated oven and cook for 8 minutes or until fish flakes. Continue to cook tomatoes until soft and crumbs are golden. To serve, transfer fish to individual plates. Pour over any pan juices. Top with roasted peppers, an anchovy fillet, and a tomato half at the side.

### Ingredients

3 large tomatoes halved across centre

salt and pepper to season

2 tbsp extra virgin olive oil

1 cup white breadcrumbs, seasoned

6 red fish fillets

1 cup dry white wine

**Marinated roast peppers**

3 large peppers, seeded and cut into 2in/5cm wide strips

½ cup extra virgin olive oil

1 tbsp chopped fresh basil

1 tsp dried oregano

4 cloves garlic, finely chopped

½ tsp salt; 6 anchovy fillets

¼ tsp freshly ground black pepper

**Baked** Red Fish with
Marinated Roast Pepper ·

**Cut** the shark into 6 even pieces. Set aside. Heat a barbecue high to medium. Pierce peppers with a knife and place on the hottest part of the grill. The skin should blister and char slightly after 12 minutes. Place in an airtight plastic bag and allow to steam and cool. When cool enough to handle, remove the skin.

**Thread** all the potatoes on metal skewers. Place them over moderate part of the barbecue. Cook for 25–30 minutes turning occasionally, and brushing with the orange vinaigrette. Add zucchini, and cook 8 to 10 min until slightly browned, but tender. Baste occasionally with orange vinaigrette.

**Add** the shark chunks, and cook for 6 min. per side. Baste occasionally with orange vinaigrette. Place radicchio halves on the barbecue. Brush with vinaigrette. Cook for 4-5 minutes, until leaves are wilted and slightly charred. Remove all vegetables and fish to a serving dish and keep hot. Pour remaining orange vinaigrette into a saucepan and bring to a boil while stirring. Drizzle over vegetables and fish, serve immediately.

## Ingredients

2lb 4oz/1kg fresh shark steaks
(cut into chunks about 1in/2.5cm-thick)
2 red or yellow peppers
(pierced once with a knife)
12 small red-skinned potatoes,
washed and halved
orange vinaigrette (recipe follows)
3 zucchini (ends trimmed)
1 head radicchio (red chicory),
sliced in half lengthwise

# **Barbecued Shark** and Vegetables with Orange Vinaigrette

**Orange Vinaigrette**

2 tbsp olive oil, 1 tbsp soy sauce

1 tsp freshly chopped ginger

1 tsp grated orange rind

1 cup freshly squeezed orange juice

2 tbsp balsamic or white wine vinegar

pinch ground cayenne pepper

1 tsp dry mustard

**Preheat** oven to moderate temperature (355°F/ 180°C). Heat oil in frying pan and sauté garlic, tomatoes and onion (until soft).

**Add** pepper, olives, thyme, tarragon, and wine. Cook, uncovered (for 5 minutes) over a moderate heat.

**Place** steaks in a greased, shallow, ovenproof dish. Pour sauce over steaks. Cover and cook in the preheated moderate oven for 20 minutes or until steaks are cooked through.

# **Baked** Snapper Niçoise

## Ingredients

1 tbsp olive oil

3 tsp freshly crushed garlic

2 ripe tomatoes, chopped

1 small onion, finely chopped

1 large red pepper, seeded and finely diced

2¼ oz/65g black olives, pitted and sliced

¼ tsp dried thyme leaves

½ tsp dried tarragon leaves

1½ cups dry white wine

4 snapper steaks

**To butterfly the trout:** remove head. Split the stomach cavity through to the tail, open out. Slide the tip of a small knife between the fine bones and flesh to free the bones. Do this in manageable groups. Snip the back bone at both ends and gently peel away from flesh beginning at head end.

**Preheat** grill. On a lightly oiled grilling pan, arrange trout, skin-side down so that they are not touching each other. Spoon about 1 tablespoon of lime juice over each fish.

**Drizzle** each with one teaspoon butter, then season with cumin, salt, and cayenne. Place under the hot grill, 4-6in/10-15cm from heat for 6-8 minutes without turning, until lightly browned and opaque throughout.

# **Grilled** Trout Calypso

## Ingredients

4 trout (each about 9oz/250g, butterflied and boned)

¼ cup fresh lime juice

1 tbsp butter, melted

½ tsp ground cumin seeds

½ tsp salt

¼ tsp ground cayenne pepper

**Preheat** oven (to 420°F/ 215°C). Set out 4 equal pieces of silicon baking paper (each about 12 x 16in/30 x 40cm), and place steaks in center of front half. Season with salt and pepper. Pour one tablespoon butter over each steak.

**Top** with five asparagus spears and spread equal amounts of pepper strips over each steak. Sprinkle each steak with one tablespoon of white wine.

**Fold** top of paper over fish to front edge and double fold edges tightly to seal. Place on a baking tray in a single layer. Bake for 15-20 minutes (until paper is puffed and steaks are cooked through).

# **Tuna** Steaks with White Wine and Asparagus

### Ingredients

4 tuna steaks (each about 5oz/150g; cut 2.5cm-thick)

½ tsp salt

¼ tsp cracked black peppercorns

4 tbsp butter (melted)

20 asparagus spears (trimmed about 4in/12cm long)

⅓ each red, yellow, and green pepper (cut into thin strips)

¼ cup white wine

**Heat** butter in small saucepan, add flour, and cook, stirring, over low heat for 1 minute.

**Remove** sauce from heat and whisk in cream, gherkins, capers, parsley and shallots. Return to heat and gently warm through. Do not allow to boil. Cover and set aside. Add the octopus and 4 cups of its cooking liquid.

**Coat** fillets in flour, then in egg and breadcrumbs. Heat oil in frying pan. Add fillets and cook 2-3 minutes each side, or until cooked through.

## Ingredients

1lb 2oz/500g whiting fillets

plain flour

2 eggs, lightly beaten

4½ oz/125g dry breadcrumbs

oil (for shallow frying)

**Warm Tartar Sauce**

4 tbsp butter

2 tbsp plain flour

2 tbsp dry white wine

½ cup water

1 cube chicken stock

1¼ cups/10fl oz/300ml heavy cream

2 gherkins, chopped

1 tbsp capers, rinsed and chopped

1 tbsp fresh chopped parsley

4 green onions, chopped

**Whiting** with Warm Tartar Sauce

**Fry** bacon in a large frypan (until crisp). Pour off almost all fat, keeping a small amount. Fry onion, garlic, celery, carrot, and chili in the remaining bacon fat. Cook for 3-4 minutes (until vegetables are tender).

**Add** the tomatoes, including the juice, tomato paste, bay leaves, thyme, and salt and pepper. Stir in the fish stock, water, abalone, and potatoes. Bring the mixture to a boil, then reduce heat to simmer. Simmer uncovered for 40-45 minutes.

**Combine** the flour, and water to a smooth paste, then pour into the chowder. Add the sherry. Stir and increase the heat (until the liquid boils). Allow the mixture to boil gently (until the broth thickens slightly). Taste for seasoning, and add more sherry, salt, and pepper (if desired).

## Ingredients

| | |
|---|---|
| 2 slices bacon, cut into 1in/2.5cm pieces | ½ tsp salt |
| 1 medium onion, chopped | ½ tsp black peppercorns (freshly ground) |
| 3 tsp freshly crushed garlic | 1 cup basic fish stock |
| 2 stalks celery, chopped | 6 cups water |
| 1 large carrot, chopped | 1lb 2oz/500g abalone steaks |
| ½ tsp freshly chopped chili | (ground or finely chopped) |
| 1lb/440g can tomato pieces | 2 medium pontiac potatoes (diced) |
| 2 tbsp tomato paste | 2 tbsp plain flour |
| 2 bay leaves | 4 tbsp water |
| 1 heaped tsp thyme leaves | ½ cup dry sherry |

# **Abalone** Chowder

fish & seafood

**To make the dressing:** place the tomatoes in a bowl and cover with boiling water. Leave for 30 seconds, then skin, deseed and cut into small dice.

**Whisk** together the oil and vinegar in a bowl, then whisk in the cream, tarragon, and seasoning. Add sugar and sauce to taste, then stir in the tomatoes and cucumber.

**Fork** over the crab meat. Mix together the crab meat and sliced fennel and stir in 4 tablespoons of the dressing. Arrange the salad leaves together with the crab mixture on plates. Spoon over the remaining dressing, then sprinkle with the chives, chopped fennel top, and paprika or cayenne pepper.

### Ingredients

9oz/250g fresh or canned crab meat

1 large bulb fennel, thinly sliced, with feathery top chopped and reserved to garnish

3oz/85g mixed salad leaves

1 tbsp snipped fresh chives and paprika or cayenne pepper to garnish

### Dressing

2 large tomatoes; 5 tbsp olive oil

1 tbsp white wine vinegar

4 tbsp single cream

1 tsp chopped fresh tarragon

salt and black pepper

pinch of caster sugar

dash of Worcestershire sauce

2in/5cm piece cucumber, diced

# **Crab** Salad with Tomato Dressing

**Remove** lobster meat from shells and cut into bite-sized pieces. Reserve shells. In a saucepan, place milk, bay leaf, onion, and peppercorns. Heat slowly to boiling point. Remove from heat, cover and stand for 10 minutes to infuse. Strain.

**Heat** butter in a pan, and remove from heat. Stir in flour and blend, gradually adding strained milk. Return pan to heat, and stir constantly (until sauce boils and thickens). Simmer sauce for 1 minute. Remove from heat, add cream, cheese, salt, and pepper. Stir sauce (until cheese melts) and add lobster.

**Divide** mixture between shells. Melt extra butter in a small pan, add breadcrumbs, and stir to combine. Scatter crumbs over lobster and brown under a hot grill.

## Ingredients

1 medium lobster, cooked and halved

**Mornay Sauce**

1¼ cup milk

1 bay leaf

1 small onion, chopped

5 whole black peppercorns

3 tbsp butter

2 tbsp plain flour

¼ cup cream

2¼ oz/65g cheese, grated

salt and cracked black peppercorns

2 tbsp extra butter, melted

2¼ oz/65g fresh breadcrumbs

**Lobster** Mornay

**Melt** butter over a moderate heat in a shallow frypan. When the foam subsides, add lobster. Cook slowly (for about 5 minutes). Add the salt, cayenne pepper and nutmeg.

**Beat** lightly the cream with the egg yolks in a small bowl. Add the mixture to the pan stirring gently on low heat. When mixture begins to thicken, stir in the brandy and sherry. Do not allow to boil.

**Serve** either (i) placed back in the lobster tail shell; or (ii) in vol-au-vent cases. Serve with steamed rice in shell (or vol-au-vent cases).

# **Lobster** Newburg

## Ingredients

6 tbsp butter

4½lb/2kg cooked lobster, halved, flesh removed and diced

2 tsp salt

¼ tsp ground cayenne pepper

¼ tsp ground nutmeg

1 cup heavy cream

4 egg yolks

2 tbsp brandy

2 tbsp dry sherry

reserved lobster-tail shell or 4-6 vol-au-vent cases and rice (for serving).

**Melt** butter over a moderate heat in a shallow frypan. Add garlic, spring onions, tomatoes and their juice, salt and pepper, and saffron. Cook until onions are translucent (about 2 minutes).

**Remove** meat from lobster, and cut into large pieces. Add lobster to frypan, and flame with the brandy. Cook gently (until lobster is heated through). Place rice on serving plate, and sprinkle with chives.

**Remove** lobster from frypan (retaining the cooking liquid as a sauce). Arrange the lobster on the rice and spoon over the sauce. Serve with lemon wedges on side of plate.

**Ingredients**

6 tbsp butter

1 tsp freshly crushed garlic

2 spring onions, chopped

11oz/300g can tomatoes, chopped

salt and cracked black peppercorns (to taste)

pinch of saffron

1 large cooked lobster

¼ cup brandy

boiled rice

½ bunch fresh chives (chopped, for garnish)

lemon wedges (for garnish)

# **Lobster** Provençale

**Put** octopus in a large sauce-pan without adding water. Sprinkle with salt, cover, and let cook in its own juices over a low heat for about 45 minutes. After 10 minutes, lift the octopus out with a fork and dip into a pan of boiling water; then run the octopus under cold water and return to the saucepan to continue cooking. Repeat process every 10 minutes, 4 times total.

**Heat** olive oil in a heatproof dish, add onions and gently fry for 1 minute. Add garlic, tomatoes with juice, and chili powder, cook for about 10 minutes. Add the potatoes and cook for about 5 min-utes. Add the octopus and its cooking liquid.

**Add** salt to taste, and cook gently, uncovered for about 20 minutes, then add the peas and cook 10 minutes more until potatoes and peas are tender and sauce is reduced. Serve the octo-pus and vegetables straight from the casserole.

# **Octopus** with Potatoes and Peas

## Ingredients

2lb 4oz/1kg octopus

⅔ cup olive oil

1 large onion (chopped)

4 cloves garlic (chopped)

salt

14oz/400g can tomatoes

¼ tsp ground chilies

1lb 2oz/500g potatoes

(peeled and cut into thick slices)

9oz/250g frozen peas, thawed

**Sprinkle** the oysters with lime juice and top with smoked salmon.

**Dollop** the sour cream onto each oyster.

**Garnish** with chives and red caviar. Serve on a bed of ice.

# **Oysters** Greta Garbo

## **Ingredients**

3 dozen natural oysters in shells

juice of ½ lime or lemon

6 slices smoked salmon (cut into fine strips)

1 cup/8oz/250ml sour cream

2 tbsp fresh chives (chopped, for garnish)

red caviar (for garnish)

crushed ice (for serving)

**Peel** and devein shrimp (leaving the shell tails intact). Combine oil, wine, shallots, lemon rind, and pepper. Mix well.

**Thread** the shrimp onto bamboo skewers (approximately 3 per skewer). Place the skewers in a shallow dish and pour over marinade. Allow to marinate for at least 1 hour.

**Roll** the shrimp in the toasted sesame seeds, pressing them on well. Refrigerate for 30 minutes before cooking. Place the shrimp skewers on a hot oiled barbecue grill and cook for 1-2 minutes on each side or until they turn pink. Brush with marinade during cooking.

**Ingredients**

2lb 4oz/1kg medium-large green king shrimp

¼ cup olive oil

¼ cup red wine

4 shallots (finely chopped)

1 tsp (grated lemon rind)

½ tsp cracked black peppercorns

12 bamboo skewers

(soaked in water for 30 minutes)

4  oz/125g toasted sesame seeds

## **Sesame** Barbecued Shrimp

**Use** the 12 scallop shells for the cooking and serving dishes. Mix the scallops with the sherry, and then place two scallops in each shell. Set aside.

**Soak** the black beans covered in cold water for 15 minutes, then rinse, dry on paper towels, and mash. Combine the beans, garlic, soy sauce, salt, pepper, sugar, oil, and cornflour. Distribute some of this mixture equally over each of the scallops, and trickle the sesame oil over each.

**Bring** a few inches of water to a vigorous boil in a steamer. Place the scallops on a steamer rack, cover tightly, and steam for 5 minutes. Remove, sprinkle with spring onions, and garnish with one coriander leaf and a hot chili diamond before serving.

# **Steamed** Scallops with Black Beans and Garlic

## Ingredients

12 large scallops on shell or 24 small scallops

1 tbsp dry sherry

1 tbsp Chinese salted black beans

1 tsp freshly crushed garlic

3 tsp soy sauce

pinch cracked black peppercorns

¼ tsp salt

½ tsp sugar

1 tsp oil

1 tsp cornflour

¼ tsp Oriental sesame oil

1 spring onion (green part only, cut into fine slices)

12 coriander leaves

½ hot chili (seeded; cut into ¼in/½cm diamond shapes)

**Heat** oil in a frying pan, add onion and garlic, then sauté until tender.

**Stir** in basil, curry paste, salt, pepper, and honey. Mix well.

**Add** the calamari rings, gently stir the calamari a few minutes (until cooked through). Stir in parsley.

# **Sautéed** Calamari

## Ingredients

3 tbsp olive oil

1 large onion (sliced)

2 tsp freshly crushed garlic

1 tbsp chopped basil leaves

1 tbsp madras mild curry

salt and freshly ground black peppercorns

1lb 2oz/500g calamari rings

1 tbsp finely chopped parsley

2 tbsp honey

**Wipe** the fish fillets, remove any scales from the skin side by scraping from the tail end with the back of a knife. Remove any fine bones with a pair of tweezers.

**Season** lightly, then press 2 sage leaves onto skin side of each fillet and wrap in a slice of prosciutto. Cover and refrigerate for 30 minutes, or up to 8 hours to allow the flavors to mingle. Heat the butter and oil in a large frying pan. Place the fish in the pan, sage-side up, and cook for 2-3 minutes. Turn over and cook for a further 2-3 minutes, until the fish is opaque and the outside crisp and deep red. Serve with lemon wedges.

## Ingredients

4 red mullet fillets, about 9oz/250g

salt and black pepper

16 fresh sage leaves

4 thin slices prosciutto crudo, such as Parma ham, halved lengthways

2 tbsp butter

2 tbsp olive oil

Lemon wedges to serve

**Red** Mullet Saltimbocca

fish & seafood

75

**Preheat** the grill to high and line the grill tray with kitchen foil. Place the salmon steaks on top and season lightly. Grill for 4-5 minutes on each side, until lightly browned and cooked through.

**To make the vinaigrette:** mix together the mint, shallot, oil, and lemon juice, then season to taste. Spoon over the salmon steaks and garnish with mint.

# **Grilled** Salmon Steaks with Mint Vinaigrette

## Ingredients

4 salmon steaks, about 6oz/175g each

salt and black pepper

**For the vinaigrette**

2 tbsp chopped fresh mint, plus extra leaves to garnish

1 small shallot, finely chopped

6 tbsp olive or vegetable oil

juice of 1 lemon

**To make the anchovy butter:** blend the anchovies, butter, lemon juice, and plenty of pepper until smooth in a food processor, or with a blender. lternatively, mash the anchovies and beat in the other ingredients with a spoon. Shape into a small roll, wrap in plastic wrap, then place in the refrigerator.

**Season** the plaice fillets and dust with the flour. Heat 1 tablespoon of oil in a large heavy-based frying pan over a high heat, add 2 plaice fillets, skin-side up, and fry for 1 minute or until golden brown.

**Turn** over and fry for 2 minutes or until browned. Remove from the pan and keep warm. Wipe out the pan with absorbant paper towel and cook the remaining fillets in the same way. Unwrap the butter roll and cut into slices, discarding the paper. Serve the fish with a slice of anchovy butter on top, garnished with chives.

# **Fried** Fillet of Plaice with Anchovy Butter

## Ingredients

4 large plaice fillets

2 tbsp plain flour

2 tbsp vegetable oil or oil
from the drained anchovies

fresh chives to garnish

**For the butter**

2oz/50g can anchovy fillets in olive oil, drained

5 tbsp unsalted butter, softened

1 tbsp lemon juice

salt and black pepper

**Mix** together the nuts and breadcrumbs in a large shallow bowl. Put the flour into another bowl and season. Put the egg into a third bowl. Dip the fish pieces into the flour, then into the egg and finally into the breadcrumb mixture to coat.

**Heat** ⅓ in/1cm of oil in a large frying pan and fry a third of the fish pieces for 5 minutes or until golden on all sides. Drain on paper towels and keep warm while you cook the rest in 2 batches. Serve with tartar sauce or sprinkled with vinegar or lemon juice.

# **Nut** Crusted Flake Bites

### Ingredients

4 tbsp chopped hazelnuts

4 tbsp fresh breadcrumbs

2 tbsp plain flour

salt and black pepper

1 large egg, beaten

1lb 2oz/500g flake fillet, cut into

20 even-sized pieces

vegetable oil for shallow frying pan

tartar sauce

vinegar or lemon juice to serve

**Cut** skate wings into 3 even pieces. Season the fish with salt and pepper. Dip into the flour to coat both sides and shake off excess.

**Heat** the oil and 2 teaspoons butter in a large nonstick frying pan over medium heat. Add the skate and fry each side for 5 minutes or until golden and cooked through at the thickest part.

**Add** the remaining butter to the pan and heat until nut brown. Slowly add the vinegar while stirring continuously. Heat well then stir in the capers and parsley. Pour immediately over the fish and serve with vegetable accompaniment.

# **Fried** Skate with Black Butter

## Ingredients

salt and black pepper

2 skate wing fillets, 8oz/225g each

2 tbsp plain flour

1 tbsp vegetable oil

4 tbsp butter

2 tbsp white wine vinegar

2 tbsp capers, drained

2 tbsp chopped fresh parsley

**Rinse** the rice thoroughly, then cook according to the packet instructions. Drain and leave to cool. Put the eggs into a saucepan of cold water. Bring to a boil and cook for 10 minutes. Cool under cold running water, then shell and chop roughly.

**Place** the kippers in a dish and cover with boiling water. Leave to stand for 5 minutes. Drain, remove the skin, roughly flake the fish and discard any visible bones.

**Melt** half the butter in a large nonstick frying pan, then add the onion and cook for 4 minutes or until softened. Add the rice and mix well, then add the eggs, kippers, parsley, lemon juice, seasoning, and the remaining butter, and heat through thoroughly.

# **Kipper** Kedgeree

### Ingredients

9oz/250g basmati rice

4 large eggs

4 smoked kipper fillets

3oz/75g butter

1 onion, finely chopped

8 tbsp chopped fresh parsley

3 tbsp lemon juice

salt and black pepper

**Make** 4 deep slashes along each side of the fish. Mix oil and soy sauce together and rub into the fish inside and out. Cover and place in the refrigerator for 30 minutes.

**Spread** half the carrot, spring onions, and ginger on a large piece of foil. Place the fish on top, then sprinkle with the remaining vegetables and ginger and any remaining marinade.

**Loosely** fold over the foil to seal. Transfer the fish to a steamer for 20 minutes or until the fish is firm and cooked through. Put the sesame oil, if using, into a small saucepan and heat. Drizzle over the fish and garnish with coriander.

### Ingredients

1 grey mullet, about
1lb 9oz/700g scaled,
gutted, and cleaned
½ tsp salt
1 tbsp vegetable oil

1 tbsp light soy sauce
1 large carrot, cut into fine strips
4 spring onions, cut into fine strips
1 tbsp grated fresh root ginger
1 tbsp sesame oil (optional)
fresh coriander to garnish

# **Chinese** Style Steamed Grey Mullet

**Heat** the oil in a wok, add the ginger and shrimp, then stir-fry for 2 minutes or until the shrimp is just turning pink.

**Add** the mangetout and spring onions and stir-fry for a further minute to soften slightly.

**Stir** in the mango and soy sauce and stir-fry for 1 minute to heat through. Serve immediately.

# **Tiger** Shrimp, Mangetout, and Mango Stir-fry

## Ingredients

2 x 7oz/200g packs frozen raw peeled tiger shrimp, defrosted, rinsed, and dried

2 tbsp vegetable oil

1½ tbsp finely grated fresh root ginger

7oz/200g mangetout, strings removed

bunch of spring onions, sliced

1 large ripe mango, peeled and thinly sliced

2 tbsp light soy sauce

**Mix** together the yogurt, chili powder, paprika, cumin, coriander, turmeric, garam masala, garlic, tomato purée, and lime juice. Place the cod in a large, shallow, non-metallic dish. Pour over the marinade and turn to cover. Cover and refrigerate for 4 hours or overnight, turning occasionally.

**Mix** cucumer and salt together, place in a strainer and stand 10 minutes, then press with the back of a spoon to press out water. To make the raita, mix together with the carrot, yogurt and mint, or coriander. Cover and refrigerate until needed.

**Preheat** the grill to high. Place the marinated cod in a shallow flameproof dish or oven tray. Place under the grill and cook for 8 minutes or until the flesh is firm and cooked through, turning once. Serve the cod with the raita.

## Ingredients

½ cup natural yogurt

1 tsp mild chili powder

1 tsp paprika

1 tsp ground cumin

½ tsp ground coriander

½ tsp turmeric

1 tsp garam masala

1 large clove garlic, crushed

1 tsp tomato purée

juice of ½ lime

1lb 9oz/700g skinless cod fillet, cut into 4 pieces

**For the raita**

1 small Lebanese cucumber, grated

¼ tsp salt

1 carrot, grated

7oz/200g carton natural yogurt

2 tbsp chopped fresh mint or coriander

## **Tandoori** Cod with Cucumber and Carrot Raita

**To prepare the butter:**

place the wine and onion in
a small saucepan and bring
to a boil. Boil rapidly for
about 4-5 minutes over
a high heat or until reduced
to about 2 tablespoons.
Remove from the heat and
allow to cool completely.

**Beat** the butter in a bowl
until smooth, add the
parsley, garlic, seasoning,
and reduced wine and mix
together with a fork. Place
the butter on a piece of
greaseproof paper and
roll up into a tight sausage
shape. Place in the
refrigerator and chill
until hardened.

**Wash** and wipe the salmon
with kitchen paper. Heat the
oil in a large frying pan over
a medium heat and cook the
salmon for 4 minutes. Turn
and cook for 3-4 minutes
more, until cooked through.
Cut the butter into four
pieces and place one on
top of each salmon fillet.
Allow the butter to melt
by cooking 2 minutes
longer before serving.

**Ingredients**

1 tbsp sunflower oil

4 salmon fillets, weighing about 6oz/175g each,
skinned

**For the butter**

⅔ cup red wine

½ small red onion, finely chopped

3oz/75g butter, softened

2 tbsp finely chopped fresh parsley,
plus extra, to garnish

1 clove garlic, very finely chopped

sea salt and freshly ground
black pepper

**Salmon** with Onion and Red Wine Butter

**Heat** half the oil in a large frying pan, swirl to cover base. Add asparagus orange rind and season with salt. Cover and cook over low heat for 2 minutes, turn asparagus, cook 2 minutes more. Remove to a plate and cover to keep hot. Clean the pan with kitchen paper.

**Wash** and wipe the salmon with paper towel and season. Heat the remaining oil in a large frying pan over a medium heat. Add the salmon to the pan and cook for 4-5 minutes each side or until golden and cooked through.

**Add** the balsamic vinegar and orange juice and simmer for about 2 minutes until the sauce is bubbling and warmed through, stir in the coriander and serve immediately with the asparagus.

# **Salmon** with Asparagus, Balsamic, and Orange

## Ingredients

2 tbsp extra virgin olive oil

finely grated rind of ½ orange, plus the juice of 1 orange

sea salt and freshly ground black pepper

9oz/250g bunch asparagus, trimmed

4 salmon steaks, weighing about 6oz/175g each

1 tbsp balsamic vinegar

2 tbsp chopped fresh coriander

# **In**dex